Liberating Faith

Bonhoeffer's Message for Today

GEFFREY B. KELLY

Introduction by Eberhard Bethge

AUGSBURG Publishing House • Minneapolis

LIBERATING FAITH
Bonhoeffer's Message for Today

Library of Congress Cataloging in Publication Data

Kelly, Geffrey B.
    LIBERATING FAITH.

    Bibliography: p.
    1. Bonhoeffer, Dietrich, 1906-1945.   I. Title.
BX4827.B57K44   1984   230'.044'0924   84-15863
ISBN 0-8066-2092-7

Manufactured in the U.S.A.   APH 10-3832

1   2   3   4   5   6   7   8   9   0   1   2   3   4   5   6   7   8   9

Contents

Church and state: tensions in ecclesiology
The church and the racial issue in the years of crisis
Church freedom, ecumenism, and the Nazi crisis
The church's critical presence in the world
A church confessing guilt: a church for others

Liberation in Christ
The "discipline of the secret": liberating religion from itself
"Nonreligious" Christianity: freedom for the Word of God
Freedom in the prayer of silence and the fellowship
    of prayer
Stations on the road to freedom: faith's liberating power

"The view from below": a challenge to the churches
Bonhoeffer and the Jews: church guilt in the Holocaust
Bonhoeffer and contemporary liberation theology
Church solidarity with the oppressed
Liberation and the criteria for violence
The cross of Christ: symbol of courage in faith

Introduction

For several decades now my wife Renate and I have endeavored to make Dietrich Bonhoeffer better known in the United States. This has involved us in an attempt to interpret the life and work of a theologian-pastor who himself was not only very German but whose theology was also deeply stamped with his Protestant Reformation thought-patterns and those experiences special to Germans and Germany, which I shared with him.

As a consequence of this project, I have become more and more convinced that in the long run an accurate interpretation would be achieved and distortions prevented only if Americans themselves would undertake a thorough investigation into Bonhoeffer's theology considered as a whole. For this to happen much additional time and research were required: a phase of obtaining accurate translations, a period of discussion by experts, and the crucial stage of debate and disputation in theses, dissertations, articles, and specialized books overflowing with enthusiasm and critical observations. In the tentative conclusions and encounters of all sorts that followed we saw an obvious need for more maturity of judgment and further growth in knowledge of the conditions and difficulties of the Nazi period. There was likewise room for analysis of the theological-ecclesial traditions as viewed by both Germans and Americans in order to understand Bonhoeffer from several possible perspectives and to achieve a truly worthwhile interpretation.

It seems that the time has finally arrived for this project to be realized. We have now before us the first book by an American that combines accurate analysis with the creation of valuable guidelines for future discussions of the critical implications of Bonhoeffer's life and theology. The author, Geffrey B. Kelly, is a well-known Bonhoeffer scholar who has himself taken part in all the stages of research and critical debate. He is proposing here neither a dissertation nor a disputation, but rather a book that could serve as a study text for all those seriously interested in the entire phenomenon of Dietrich Bonhoeffer.

From his preface we can learn of his practical research into and proper evaluation of the sources as well as his appreciation of Bonhoeffer himself which Dr. Kelly has incorporated into his interpretation. It appears to me that this work is endowed with three converging qualities that make it valuable for both specialists and the general public. These qualities are indicative of a reliable writer whose conclusions we can thoroughly trust. Dr. Kelly combines the skills of a theologian with the art of storyteller and the gifts of a good teacher.

First of all, the author is recognized as one of the most respected interpreters of Bonhoeffer's theological legacy. In reading his book, one experiences the superb skill with which he has mastered the wide-ranging subject matter. This he has integrated into a coherent unity under that striking title, *Liberating Faith*. He does not allow himself to be distracted by those sensational catchphrases that dominated earlier American attempts to interpret Bonhoeffer and made those efforts so incomplete and slanted. Nor does he fail to keep a balance between the larger theological tradition and sensitivity for the contemporary period which Bonhoeffer represents. As a Catholic theologian, the author has been trained in basic Christian spirituality, to which he brings his own sharp theological logic. His expertise in the American church situation is also far-reaching. He has thereby gained a deeper appreciation of what for him were those inspiring and liberating sentences on "cheap grace" in Bonhoeffer's *The Cost of Discipleship*. Dr. Kelly is also thoroughly familiar with the world of the German Reformation, which is the proper background of Bonhoeffer's theology, as of the German church struggle, which is the immediate setting of those crises which shaped that theology. His evident familiarity with the present status of national and international discussions on these issues adds to the importance of his analysis.

What is more, this distinguished and reliable scholar has decided to write, as he puts it, a study of Bonhoeffer's life and writings that will stress the positive. This he promises in his preface, with that wit which is so uniquely his: "I have no intention here of trying, with the teeth of theological criticism, to pick the bones of Bonhoeffer's theology clean of any weak elements or inconclusive assertions .... This book is not a quarrel with Bonhoeffer and his critics." It is not that Kelly would suppress the necessary critical distance where such appears indispensable for the correct understanding of a point. Rather, he addresses himself to his readers in a way that is ultimately more genuine. He is not competing in an exhibition match with other interpreters, who, for the most part, seem to engage in intellectual duels merely for the sake of argument. On the contrary, he narrates theology in its biographical and historically conditioned complexity with fidelity to the richness of the various traditions—certainly not a simple undertaking—but only to involve the reader in a drama of faith seriously pondered and courageously lived. This is reflected in the short but authentic and inspiring life of Bonhoeffer during a fatal period of his country and his church.

And what may be of special value to readers, this scholarly theologian and storyteller shows that he is a gifted and skillful teacher with considerable experience in teaching religion at all levels of education. He sums up each of his demanding chapters with a series of study questions. These stimulate the individual reader or discussion groups to examine their personal understanding of the events and issues and to express their own opinions. Where necessary, one is led to investigate Bonhoeffer's unique theological and historical connections with the modern period, particularly in view of the current resurgence of the same problems that caused the Nazi crisis in church and world.

Finally, it is gratifying to be able to recognize in this book an important contribution to Bonhoeffer studies. The author has not given us another exercise in theological hairsplitting. Instead, this is a fascinating book by a scholar of note that will be instructive for the English speaking world. It brings together all the elements of what is central to the experience of liberation and convincingly exposes the secret of Bonhoeffer's own dialectic of freedom and obligation in his life and thought. This experience has also freed the author to make some demands on his readers. Bonhoeffer himself is hardly "easy" in his demands, if one would be led by his example and inspiration to conversion or to make a more serious commitment in one's faith. To such an end, this book is an immense help. In particular, it helps us better to understand why and how Bonhoeffer belongs not only to Germany but to all Christians in the world, and why and how his voice will continue to be heard in the future.

DR. EBERHARD BETHGE
BONN
FEDERAL REPUBLIC OF GERMANY

Preface

My encounter with Dietrich Bonhoeffer began in the summer of 1964 when I was spiritual director of a group of postulants in the novitiate of the Christian Brothers. While browsing in their religious reading library, I noticed, by pure chance, the attractive title of a new book on the shelves, Dietrich Bonhoeffer's *The Cost of Discipleship*. I opened the book at random to the startling sentence: "We . . . have gathered like eagles round the carcass of cheap grace, and there we have drunk of the poison which has killed the life of following Christ." [1] This seemed on that day to be the inspiring yet perplexing word I needed for my uneasy mood. I sensed almost immediately that I too had been pursuing the "cheap grace" of a religious routine. Reading, I became utterly fascinated by the awesome demands of the Sermon on the Mount, which through Bonhoeffer's words seemed to be addressed to me for the first time. I resolved to learn more about this author and, like so many others, was led to the prison letters and the story of his execution. Even today

I am as deeply moved by the challenges of these letters as by the personal sacrifice of their author.

The opportunity to engage in a systematic study of the life and writings of Bonhoeffer did not come until 1967, when I was assigned to pursue doctoral studies in theology in Louvain, Belgium. There I was fortunate to work under the noted professor of dogmatic theology, Adolphe Gesché, who had himself been long interested in the issues of both revelation theology in general and of Bonhoeffer's radical challenge to the churches and to the people exercising leadership in those churches. Much research was needed in each area. Professor Gesché's willingness to direct that research made it possible for me to pursue my interest in Bonhoeffer and in the whole question of the interrelationship of revelation, faith, and church.

One pleasant aspect of that research was the opportunity it gave me to meet the Bonhoeffer family and friends, particularly Eberhard and Renate Bethge. Eberhard was Bonhoeffer's best friend and confessor, the recipient of the prison letters, editor of the posthumous writings, and author of the definitive biography, which George Steiner, writing for the *New York Times*, has described as "one of the few assured classics of our age." Renate is Bonhoeffer's niece and the daughter of a coconspirator against Hitler, Rüdiger Schleicher, who was himself also murdered by the S.S. in the closing days of the war. The Bethges provided me with many of the unpublished documents which I was then able to incorporate into my own work. Through Eberhard I was able to confirm many of the hunches I had about the sources of Bonhoeffer's writings, such as the influence of Kierkegaard on Bonhoeffer's *The Cost of Discipleship*. What is more important, in Eberhard I felt I had indeed come close to the person who had most helped to shape the insights of this modern martyr. Elsewhere I have expressed the hope that someday some enterprising student of Bonhoeffer's theology would write a definitive study of Bethge's influence on Bonhoeffer, an influence only hinted at but hardly developed in my own dissertation. Somehow I sensed that I had encountered Bonhoeffer himself through the attractive personality of his biographer and friend.

On return trips to Louvain I have been asked repeatedly by my professors when I am going to publish my dissertation. The truth is that I have already published several sections of it in learned journals, and I will allude to these in the course of this book. I have always felt, though, that a two-volume thesis is not only overweight in sheer size but also too heavy in what I like to call "hard-core" theology. Not that this present book is without some well-needed theological distinctions and critical assessments of Bonhoeffer's thought that, I hope, will counter many of the more popular misinterpretations and commercializations of Bonhoeffer's theological legacy. But I have no intention here of trying, with the teeth of theological criticism, to pick the bones of Bonhoeffer's theology clean of any weak elements or inconclusive assertions. My desire is, rather, to present Bonhoeffer's probing of Christian faith in as affirmative a manner as possible. I do not apologize for the positive tone of this assessment of his theology and spirituality. This book is not a quarrel with Bonhoeffer and his critics, so much as an attempt to stress the positive challenge to Christianity which we discover in his life and writings.

My experience in giving countless talks, workshops, and courses on Bonhoeffer, dictated the type of book I wanted to write. Wherever I had lectured on Bonhoeffer I encountered a hunger for the liberating word of the Sermon on the Mount and the gospel of Christ's sufferings for us as these were embodied in Bonhoeffer's career and in his extensive writings. We live in an age when many people still desire to commit themselves to a responsible life of love and sacrifice on behalf of people both within and without their communities of faith. The groups I encountered in my lectures were religious sisters and brothers, as well as adult education audiences within parishes; they were

Protestant as well as Catholic seminarians; they were alienated college students and committed-to-Christ retreatants; they were teachers of youth as well as missionaries in countries beset by national movements to liberate people from oppression. They were people who, for the most part, wanted some kind of "life together in Christ." This book is the outgrowth of what we shared together in my lectures, in the discussions which followed, and in the moments of prayerful reflection on the meaning of a life totally centered on the person of Christ.

The title of this book is the same as the theme I have seen emerging from Bonhoeffer's life and from those reflections: the liberating faith that we experience in our encounters with Jesus Christ. Bonhoeffer's question, "Who is Jesus Christ really for us today?," is as fitting now as it was on that April day in his last year of life. Because I see this book as a text that could facilitate reflections that might lead to a deepening of our faith commitment to Christ and his gospel, I have included at the end of each chapter a series of discussion questions. Many of these spring from my encounters with the groups mentioned above. I hope that readers will be confronted in the pages that follow with Christ's call to liberation through discipleship, love for people, and the deeds of responsibility in freedom for others that inspirited the mission of Christ to the world and that became the inspiration behind Bonhoeffer's Christian commitment and his eventual martyrdom.

To the extent that this book may help us see the sources of our own Christ-centered liberation for service to others, I am indebted to many people, particularly those who have helped me sharpen my understanding of Bonhoeffer's life and legacy. I wish especially to thank Eberhard and Renate Bethge for their help in my research and for their warm hospitality during my visits to their home in West Germany. Any accuracy in my interpretation of Bonhoeffer is due to the documentation provided by the Bethges and the foundations set in Eberhard's own masterly interpretations.

It was through the Bethges that I met Dr. Clifford Green, an Australian scholar now recognized as one of the foremost experts in Bonhoeffer's theology in the English speaking world. Together with John Godsey, author of the first book in English on Bonhoeffer's theology, and Larry Rasmussen, whose study *Reality and Resistance* is a "classic" analysis of Bonhoeffer's ethics, we met in 1973 to establish what is now known as "The International Bonhoeffer Society, English Language Section." This group has grown to more than 200 members, mostly from North America, and is now affiliated with the American Academy of Religion. As we soon discovered, the Society became, especially for the inner-core of active members, a community of friends who are able to share not only scholarly interests but a genuine concern for each other that cuts across the boundaries of religion. Our national annual meetings and periodic international conferences seem as much pleasant occasions for renewing friendships as for spearheading significant research into Bonhoeffer's theology. My "brothers and sisters" in the Bonhoeffer Society are too numerous to mention here; many of their names appear in the notes. For their support, which ranges from critical research to our mutual bond of faith and love, I am grateful.

I am likewise indebted to my mentor at Louvain, Professor Adolphe Gesché, who carefully guided my original dissertation to its final form. Student meetings with Gesché were always an event, as much because of his warm personal interest in "budding theologians" as for the way he could prod students to think creatively. For me it was a special privilege to study under him.

That my research ever took presentable shape within the time set for my return to the United States can be attributed also to the helpful, cheerful community spirit of Brother Luke Salm, who lived at our religious home during his sabbatical leave at Louvain in 1971-72. Luke's constructive suggestions on the revision of the typescript, as well as the many valuable insights we shared on the nature of revelation theology, made it possible for me to compose a coherent thesis acceptable to Louvain's Major School of Theology. What is more, I am personally grateful for the scholarly encouragement which Luke has given me over the years of our friendship. Luke is typical of the Christian Brothers with whom I had been associated for so many years at La Salle College and in the Baltimore Province. It is to these religious professionals in the field of education with whom I lived as a Brother that I owe my own training in spirituality and any success I have experienced as a teacher and writer. Finally my thoughts turn to the one whose love and support have nurtured me through the difficult final stages of publication, my wonderful wife, Joan. To Joan and Luke and the Christian Brothers I dedicate this book with affection and gratitude.

1

Bonhoeffer: A Witness to Christ

In reminiscing about his friendship with Dietrich Bonhoeffer, Bishop George Bell of Chichester recalled that Bonhoeffer and the courageous people of the resistance were a moral force for a new Germany in which the fundamental principles of Christian faith would drive out the evil forces of Hitlerism and the Nazi lust for aggression. He recalled, too, Bonhoeffer's farewell message, delivered through fellow prisoner, Captain Payne Best: "I believe in the principle of our universal Christian brotherhood which rises above all national interest." [1] Bonhoeffer's belief in Christ's centrality to brotherhood and sisterhood in a world community freed to transcend racial, religious, and national divisions led him into the anti-Hitler conspiracy and to his eventual execution. Bonhoeffer was hanged by the S.S. on April 9, 1945, in the waning days of World War II. He was only 39 years old at his death, his influence on the church in Germany seemingly at an end. Yet today, a generation and a half later, Christians are still inspired by his letters and papers from prison and by the disturbing challenge to a genuine and courageous faith posed by his life and writings. In many ways Bonhoeffer has been more influential after his martyrdom than he was in his brief teaching and preaching career in Berlin during the years before his participation in the German resistance movement.

Bonhoeffer stands, moreover, as a transitional figure in the history of theology, a modern theologian and pastor who pointed to a new phase in Christian thinking that would involve a realistic questioning of all the traditional presuppositions of religion and faith. Many of the original expressions associated with Bonhoeffer, such as "costly grace," the "world-come-of-age," "worldly Christianity," "nonreligious Christianity," the "nonreligious interpretation of biblical concepts," Jesus, "the man for others," have become bywords in theology today. Bonhoeffer's prison letters encouraged Christians to question seriously the value systems of a thoroughly secularized society in order to enter into critical dialog with those who espouse attitudes and movements contrary to the Christian gospel. He has also reminded Christians of their duty to live responsibly in wholehearted, Christ-oriented service for others. In this lies the principal credibility of the Christian life. The rethinking of all the theological concepts that we have more or less taken for granted and the renewal of the church in a more human direction through the witness of unselfish service are an effort to cope with the challenge posed by his theological-pastoral legacy. Part of the continued fascination with Bonhoeffer stems from the fact that his own life and heroic death are a witness to the sincerity of his teaching.

Honesty in words and genuineness of life were attitudes especially fostered in Bonhoeffer's home. He was born in Breslau into the upper-middle-class family of Karl Bonhoeffer, the noted neurologist and professor of psychiatry at the University of Berlin, and Paula von Hase, daughter of a chaplain at the Emperor's court and granddaughter of the famous church historian, Karl von Hase, an outspoken man who was once incarcerated in the imperial prison for subversive activities. Bonhoeffer's biographer, Eberhard Bethge, reports that Dietrich's parents provided an atmosphere of love and trust for their children and instilled in them a consideration for the rights of others, a sense of self-discipline, and an openness to cultural values. Karl Bonhoeffer encouraged his children to think with precision and to decide about their own lives with complete freedom. It was this respect for the freedom and growth to maturity of his children that restrained him from voicing his misgivings when Dietrich, at the age of fourteen, announced his decision to become a pastor-theologian. At that time, the older Bonhoeffer thought the life of a theologian promised something too quiet and uneventful for his son. Once he had come to appreciate Dietrich's opposition to Hitler, which he shared, and his son's courageous role in the dangerous church crisis of 1934, he admitted that he had been ironically mistaken.[2] With his brothers, though, it was different. They manifested their disdain for Dietrich's decision by suggesting he would be squandering his talents, more suited to the noble professions undertaken by his father and themselves (one would become a physicist; another, a lawyer) for the service of a boring, petty, bourgeois institution. Bonhoeffer would later agree that the church could be both petty and bourgeois. But his reply to them—"In that case, I shall reform it" [3]—would prove strangely prophetic, at least for that small segment of the church that could take his opinions seriously.[4]

Bonhoeffer the student

Dietrich was a brilliant student, a competent musician, and a successful athlete in track and tennis. After one year of training under the famous exegete Adolf Schlatter at Tübingen, he moved on to Berlin University, where he came under the influence of the distinguished church historian Adolf von Harnack, the Luther scholar Karl Holl, and the dogmatician Reinhold Seeberg. At the surprising age of twenty-one, he had already completed his doctoral dissertation, published as a book in 1930 under the title, *Sanctorum Communio*. Later, Karl Barth would praise this work as a "theological miracle." [5] Indeed, the full title of the book, *A*

Dogmatic Inquiry into the Sociology of the Church, shows a basic interest and spiritual search that would stay at the center of Bonhoeffer's reflections to the very end of his life: to discover the concrete, communal locus of the Christian life. In this first of his books Bonhoeffer defined the church as a reality in which "Christ exists as community." [6] Hence he insisted that only in Christ does the Christian find a total interrelation of the person and the community. Bonhoeffer's thesis so closely links Christ and the church that, for him, to be "in Christ" is the same as to be in the church. In this thesis he also attempted to move between two ideas: the church as a human society and the church as the kingdom of God. The church is neither an ideal society nor a gathering of the gifted. It is an existing human reality, the result of God's action in history and as much a communion of sinners as a communion of saints touched by the saving acts of Christ.

After a lengthy trip to Rome and a year spent as pastor to a German speaking parish in Barcelona, Bonhoeffer wrote *Act and Being*, his *Habilitationsschrift*, the second dissertation required to secure a professorial appointment in German universities. Much of this second thesis, published in 1931, continues the insight of *Sanctorum Communio* that the proper understanding of revelation needs to be grounded within the church. Solely from within a concrete revelational experience can a person judge himself to have been brought by God into an interpersonal relationship with Christ. Bonhoeffer opposes any philosophical or theological system that would push God into a supratemporal sphere or that would accentuate God's freedom *over and against* people. In this he clashed with Karl Barth, a theologian whom he would come to admire the most in the years of the Nazi crisis. According to Bonhoeffer, Barth had stressed too much God's eternal elusiveness in describing the creator's relationship with creatures. On the contrary, God has "freely bound himself to historical man, having placed himself at man's disposal" ... God is free *for* man...." [7]

Before undertaking the university teaching career that approval of *Act and Being* had secured for him, Bonhoeffer accepted the Sloane Fellowship to spend a year at Union Theological Seminary in New York. The experiences of this "sabbatical year" were profoundly to affect his entire theological outlook, despite what he at the time detected to be an absence of theological substance at Union. What Bonhoeffer did find at this American seminary, on the other hand, was a deep concern for the social gospel, a desire to bring Christianity into daily contact with the everyday community. At Union, too, he formed lasting friendships with fellow students Frank Fisher and Jean Lasserre.[8] Fisher, one of the few black students at the seminary, introduced Dietrich to Christian life in Harlem's black community. Soon Bonhoeffer began to take an active part in Fisher's church and often led Sunday school groups and Bible classes. He became fascinated with the black community's "spirituals," which later he would teach to his seminaries in Finkenwalde. Lasserre, a French student-pastor, was an intensely committed pacifist, who by the force of his own faith and convictions won Bonhoeffer away from his aristocratic nationalism and enabled him not only to take a more detached view toward Germany but also to become a promoter of world peace at future ecumenical conferences. Bethge appropriately calls this period of Bonhoeffer's life a turning point in which Bonhoeffer the theologian became a Christian. Looking back on this period of his past, Bonhoeffer wrote to a friend: "For all my abandonment, I was quite pleased with myself. Then the Bible, and in particular, the Sermon on the Mount, freed me from that. Since then everything has changed . . . . It was a great liberation." [9]

The teacher and ecumenist

On his return to Germany Bonhoeffer was caught up in the political and ecclesiastical turmoil then raging as Hitler was making his strongest grab for power. Bonhoeffer's newly experienced freedom, set now in Nazism's ideological and spiritual conflict with his academic, ecumenical, and pastoral ministry, catalyzed his conviction that effective work in the church demanded his total commitment to renew the church in self-sacrificing service and to challenge it to relevance, even at the risk of its suppression by the civil authorities.

In this connection, Bonhoeffer's experience as student chaplain of the Technical University at Charlottenburg and as catechist for a confirmation class in the Zion parish in the Wedding section of Berlin gave him a lasting insight into the practical difficulties of preaching the Word to young people hardly conditioned by either social environment or personal upbringing to anything smacking of religion. The lads he had been preparing for confirmation were living in one of the poorer sections of Berlin and had already been exposed to the drums of Hitler's Youth Movement. Bonhoeffer's method with them was a free departure from the catechism then in vogue. As he disclosed in a letter to his Swiss friend Erwin Sutz:

> It is something new to them to be given something other than learning the catechism. I have developed all my instructions on the idea of the community, and these young men, who are always listening to party political speeches, know quite well what I'm getting at. . . . And again and again we have found our way from faith in the communion of saints to the forgiveness of sins, and I believe that they have now grasped something of it.[10]

In teaching the Christian message to these spiritually deprived boys, Bonhoeffer felt the necessity of interpreting the Word in terms they could understand, beyond the conventional limits of the catechism. He also recognized the need for a more active involvement in their difficulties. Therefore, he moved into their neighborhood, visited the families, invited the boys to spend weekends at a rented house in the peaceful surroundings of Biesenthal, and tried to remain in contact with them until the circumstances of war made it impossible. Years after the war, one of these students wrote:

> Our class, then, was fortunate to have such a man as its teacher. What do boys of that age normally care about the greatness of a man? But we may have felt something of it even then. He was so composed that it was easy for him to guide us; he made us familiar with the catechism in quite a new way, making it alive for us by telling us of many personal experiences. Our class was hardly ever restless because all of us were keen to have enough time to hear what he had to say to us.[11]

In addition to his practical work of preaching and teaching, Bonhoeffer's peripatetic ecumenical activities broadened his concept of the church and prepared for his scathing denunciation of the church's weakness in the face of the evil of Nazism. As Youth Secretary for the World Alliance of Churches, he traveled to conferences held in places as wide apart as England, Czechoslovakia, and Scandinavia. At the various conferences Bonhoeffer grappled with the issue of one's community in and with Jesus Christ despite the international conflicts that threatened peace in the world. He attacked not only nationalism but the vague, pusillanimous placebos issued by the churches on major issues affecting the relationship between nations and between the churches themselves. More and more he became the interpreter of the church situation in Germany to the leaders of the various national groups. He continued to prod the World Alliance to take up the challenge of becoming one church.[12]

Despite his efforts, however, it soon became clear that nationalistic interests were playing too great a role in the life of Christianity. Not only were the churches speechless before the rising militarism in Nazi Germany and the hatred and mistrust existing among so-called Christian nations, but often enough they were willing to overlook patent abuses of basic human rights in order to avoid being suppressed should they protest too loudly. The church, Bonhoeffer demanded, must not just condemn wars in general. It must condemn *this war*.[13]

The church struggle

Bonhoeffer's difficulties with the Nazi regime dated to the beginning of the Nazi takeover. On the very day after Hitler became chancellor, Bonhoeffer gave a radio broadcast on the concept of true leadership. He spoke on the *"Führer* principle" and warned against associating absolute obedience with the concept of leadership. It was dangerous, he said, to demand allegiance to the person as well as to the office since a *Führer* or leader could easily become a *Verführer* or an idol-like seducer.[14] At this juncture he was cut off the air in what may have been one of the earliest official governmental suppressions of free speech by the Nazis.

Bonhoeffer's known opposition to Nazism stiffened when Hitler, helped by some enthusiastic Nazis among the churchmen themselves, attempted to integrate Nazi racism, militarism, and imperialism with the gospel. This led to the heresy that was to split the Protestant churches into several warring factions within Germany. Those who adopted national socialism as part of their creed became known as German Christians; their church, the German Reich church. Hermann Grüner, a spokesman for the "German Christians," made it clear what this national church stood for. In one of his six theses of 1934, he had stated: "The time is fulfilled for the German people in Hitler. It is because of Hitler that Christ, God the helper and redeemer, has become effective among us. Therefore National Socialism is positive Christianity in action." Even more startling was the second thesis: "Hitler is the way of the Spirit and the will of God for the German people to enter the Church of Christ. With the courage of Luther, we German Christians strive now to build the Church with the ancient tested stones (Bible and Creed) and with the new stones (Race and People)." [15]

Led by Martin Niemoeller, Karl Barth, and Bonhoeffer, the Lutheran-Evangelical Church made its first public protest in September of 1933 at the National Synod of Wittenberg. They called for freedom to preach and freedom for the preacher. With the backing of some 2000 ministers, those assembled formed the "Confessing Church" in Germany. At the Free Synod of Barmen in May 1934 they also issued the famous "Statement of Faith" (known as the Barmen Declaration) in which Hitler's anti-Christian policies and interference with the church were denounced. One important clause in the declaration made many of the signers marked men with the Gestapo: "We repudiate the false teaching that there are areas of our life in which we belong not to Jesus Christ, but to other lords." [16] But too many pastors and their parishioners were cowed into silence or acquiescence by the terror tactics of the Nazis.

When the German Christians won controlling power over the church after the infamous "Brown Synod" of 1933, Bonhoeffer, in protest, took leave from his teaching duties at the university and went to London to serve as pastor of two German speaking parishes.[17] He was accused by his friend Karl Barth of retreating from the battlefield just when he was needed most.[18] This was not wholly accurate, because in England Bonhoeffer attempted to serve the cause of the Confessing Church by informing his fellow ministers in the Anglican church about the true nature of the German Reich church. At that time, few outside Germany had any idea of the struggle going on within the German Protestant churches.

In the meetings of the World Alliance of Churches Bonhoeffer also became known as a young radical for pestering the members to unseat the Reich church delegation and to declare them heretical. He was uncompromising on this point and also on his proposal that the churches advocate disarmament and pacifism. For Bonhoeffer, the Barmen Declaration was a justification of his view that the clash between the Confessing Church and the German Reich church was, in fact, the struggle of truth against heresy. The failure of the World Alliance to get beyond harmless theological discussions and nonthreatening definitions of the church eventually led to Bonhoeffer's disillusionment with the group and his resignation after the Youth Commission meetings of February 16-24, 1937.[19] Given the rampant nationalism of the French, Italian, and Reich church delegates, his unbending demands concerning church representation as well as the resolutions he wanted adopted and implemented appeared naive even to many of his friends.[20]

Director of an illegal seminary

As Hitler's tyranny and his hatred of Christianity became more evident, Bonhoeffer had to decide how best to resist. At this time he was impressed with Mahatma Gandhi's theories of passive resistance and nonviolent opposition to an unjust regime. Still wondering how to apply these novel ideas to Christianity and the coming moment of more open efforts to topple the Nazi government, he made arrangements to visit Gandhi in India.[21] He would have undertaken the journey. However, in the meantime, representatives of the Confessing Church persuaded him to return to Germany to assume the dangerous mission of directing an illegal seminary for young ministers who were willing to defy the Nazi ban on all ordinations within the Confessing Church. This was a job as much in line with Bonhoeffer's skills as a teacher and spiritual director as with his zest for adventure. He organized the seminary first in Zingst and later at a rambling schoolhouse in Finkenwalde near Stettin.

In a Germany geared for war, Bonhoeffer's seminary was described as an oasis of peace and spiritual freedom. The community began each morning with prayer and meditation. Their life together included daily prayers, personal confession, Bonhoeffer's own lectures, and discussions on preaching and the spiritual life.

It was a regimen considered by some of the seminarians as a bit strict.[22] He had to defend his manner of directing the seminary against critics who were quick to see in the "common life" lived there and in the "House of Brothers" the inroads of "catholicizing" tendencies in Bonhoeffer's outlook and program. Hence, he wrote:

> . . . the brethren have to learn during their short time in the seminary . . . how to lead a communal life in daily and strict obedience to the will of Christ Jesus, in the exercise of the humblest and highest service one Christian brother can perform for another; they must learn to recognize the strength and liberation to be found in brotherly service and communal life in a Christian community.[23]

The young ministers found the period of meditation difficult. Yet, on this point, too, Bonhoeffer was insistent. Even at the height of the war years he stressed again the prime importance of daily meditation in a circular letter to the brethren, many of whom were then serving on the front:

> The daily, silent meditation upon the Word of God with which I am concerned—even if it is only for a few minutes—must be for me the crystallization of everything that brings order into my life, both inwardly and outwardly. In these days when our old rules of life have had to be discarded, and there is great danger of finding our inner order endangered by the rush of events, and by the all-absorbing demands of work and service, meditation gives our life a kind of stability, maintaining a link with our earlier life, from baptism to confirmation and ordination, preserving us in the saving fellowship of our community, our brothers, and our spiritual home.[24]

The Gestapo finally turned attention to the seminary and closed it down in 1937. Bonhoeffer tried to keep the training of ministers going by shifting locations, but this "seminary on the run" proved too difficult to accomplish, because the Nazis began to conscript the young ministers. The Confessing Church, too, was beginning to waver in its refusal to compromise with the regime. Hitler had, in fact, made some concessions to the church leaders and toned down the propaganda in an effort to woo the churches over prior to unleashing his armies against Europe. Patriotism and peace were the bait.

The costly grace of discipleship

The spirit of Finkenwalde was to reach the outside world, however, through two of Bonhoeffer's books. *Life Together* describes the experience of brotherhood at the seminary and how he and his seminarians had been brought together by their vocation in Christ and by the common life they led. Their life of prayer, silent meditation on the Scriptures, hymn singing, study, and mutual service were to be the brotherly support needed for their mission to the world. This might even include possible martyrdom. *The Cost of Discipleship*, which grew out of his lectures to the seminarians and his private reflections on the gospel, is an uncompromising call to a courageous faith in the midst of the Nazi crisis. It was also a challenge rooted in Bonhoeffer's own experience of faith based on living out the Sermon on the Mount. He had written of this in a letter to his brother Karl Friedrich:

> I now believe . . . I am at last on the right track—for the first time in my life. And that often makes me very glad. . . . I believe I know that inwardly I shall be really clear and honest with myself only when I have begun to take seriously the Sermon on the Mount. . . . There are things for which an uncompromising stand is worthwhile. And it seems to me that peace and social justice, or Christ himself, are such things.[25]

In this book Bonhoeffer indicted Christians for pursuing "cheap grace," a reduction of Christianity in which grace became a principle or system, faith became intellectual assent, and the Christian life itself a somnolent gliding along with the world's standards. Christians lured into a seeming bargain of forgiveness without sincere repentance, and Baptism without commitment, lead a life hardly distinguished in its mediocrity from the rest of the world. This is "cheap grace" without discipleship, without Jesus Christ and his cross. Christians, on the contrary, are summoned to an active, self-sacrificing service, to a life of "costly grace." [26] At any moment a disciple of Christ must be ready to die for his faith after the manner of Jesus.

Work in the German resistance

Soon Bonhoeffer took the first of the decisions that would lead him to his own death for Christ. Early in the summer of 1939 he accepted the invitation of Reinhold Niebuhr to conduct a lecture tour in America. The sponsors of Bonhoeffer's trip also planned that he remain in the States to serve as pastor for German refugees in New York. The reason for this extraordinary step was Bonhoeffer's avowed intention to refuse military service and the knowledge that this would lead to possible imprisonment and perhaps a stronger repression of the Confessing Church. He decided to go to New York, therefore, to avoid this dilemma. He stayed less than a month. War was about to break out and he was tormented by the thought of his own isolation from his people when so much needed to be done to help Christianity combat Nazism.

He returned to Germany after having written a very moving letter to his American patron, Niebuhr. In this letter, which became a farewell note to his American friends, he confessed: "I have had the time to think and to pray about my situation and that of my nation and to have God's will for me clarified. I have come to the conclusion that I have made a mistake in coming to America. I must live through this difficult period of our national history with the Christian people of Germany. I will have no right to participate in the reconstruction of Christian life in Germany after the war if I do not share the trials of this time with my people." [27]

On his return Bonhoeffer initially had no legitimate base of operation. In 1940 he was forbidden to preach and told to report regularly to the police. The following year his books were proscribed and he was forbidden to write or publish. Convinced now that submission to the state in the name of a conscience unsullied by violence made one an accomplice in the "great masquerade of evil," he decided to join the anti-Nazi underground. Its center was the *Abwehr*, the German military intelligence organization. He had connections there through his brother Klaus and his brother-in-law, Hans von Dohnanyi (both later executed by the S.S.), who were eager to recruit him for their "espionage operations." His employment as a "spy" for the Third Reich also gained him the coveted exemption from the military draft.

His ostensible job was to gather intelligence material through his ecumenical contacts. Under cover of this intelligence work and because in the beginning of the war the *Abwehr* was relatively free from Gestapo surveillance, he was able to continue his writings in secret and to travel outside Germany on behalf of the resistance. His principal mission was to seek terms of surrender from the Allies if the plot against Hitler succeeded. Eventually, however, the Gestapo's jealousies and suspicions of the *Abwehr* and the actual capture of an agent in the act of smuggling Jews out of Germany led to the arrest and imprisonment of all the key figures, including the leaders, Admiral Wilhelm Canaris and General Hans Oster, and Bonhoeffer himself. At first, the Gestapo had only vague charges against them; the full truth emerged only after the failure of the July 20 assassination attempt.

The prison letters

It was from Tegel prison in Berlin that Bonhoeffer's most poignant statements about Christianity were written. Earlier, in a draft of his *Ethics* he had argued that many of the church's traditional approaches to problems were like "rusty swords," powerless against evils like Nazism. Now in the letters written during his imprisonment he proceeded to engage in a radical reappraisal of all religious structures and theological language and their relationship to the deeper meaning of Christianity. "What is bothering me incessantly," he wrote in the letter of April 30, 1944, "is the question what Christianity really is, or indeed who Christ really is, for us today." [28]

In trying to answer that question, Bonhoeffer criticized not simply the traditional images of God but especially the weak attitude of the church so pietistically wrapped up in the world beyond that it could ignore the evil of Nazi terrorism and thus compromise its integrity and relevance. Encrusted with the paraphernalia of religiosity, the church had rendered itself ineffective against the world crisis created by Hitler. The preached word issuing from such a church had become incredible to modern man and woman. Hence Bonhoeffer demanded a thoroughgoing reassessment of what really constitutes the church and how this church can effectively mediate God's presence in Christ to a "world come of age," characterized as "nonreligious."

Bonhoeffer's prototype for restructuring the church, like his entire ecclesiology, is basically Christocentric. His concern that the church answer the challenge of the mature world translates itself into a vision of Christianity in which Christ's presence in the church can once again be effectively mediated to people. This aim he enunciated in his letter of June 30, 1944. "Let me briefly summarize what I am concerned about: How is the world come of age claimed by Jesus Christ?" [29] Bonhoeffer never doubted the lordship of Christ over the world; at issue was the proper, contemporaneous understanding of this lordship after which the church could pattern itself. When the church could discover this form and live as Christ in the world, then and only then could Christ reach out through the church to his people.

This explains Bonhoeffer's keen disappointment with the Confessing Church when he observed in it the same defects which had corrupted the German Reich church. The Confessing Church, he claimed, had also forgotten that its vocation to mediate God's love demanded an active will to live as Christ and not to engage in a frantic effort to ensure its own survival. In prison Bonhoeffer perceived more clearly that Christ had always broken out of systems and institutions that wanted to hem him in. But he also saw with sadness that the church, instead of being the *alter Christus* to the world, had cowered behind its own structures, afraid to take risks that might upset the political status quo and bring on its own suppression. The future of the church, he held, depended on whether it had the courage to participate in the full life and even death of Christ in the world.

Martyrdom

In October 1944 Bonhoeffer was suddenly transferred to the Gestapo's maximum security prison. On February 7 he and 19 other "distinguished" prisoners were taken to Buchenwald. Among the prisoners was the British Intelligence office Captain Payne Best who in his book *The Venlo Incident* noted:

> Bonhoeffer was all humility; he always seemed to me to diffuse an atmosphere of happiness, of joy in every smallest event in life, and of deep gratitude for the mere fact that he was alive. He was one of the very few men that I have ever met to whom his God was real and ever close to him.[30]

Bonhoeffer and Best were among those prisoners who on April 3 were herded into a prison van and brought southward to the extermination camp at Flossenburg. By April 8 they had reached the small Bavarian village of Schönberg and there disembarked at the small schoolhouse, then being used as a temporary jail. Since it was the Sunday after Easter, several of the prisoners prevailed on Bonhoeffer to conduct a meditation service on the Bible verses for the day. First he offered Isaiah's words, "With his wounds we are healed." Then he gave the opening portion of the First Epistle of Peter, "Blessed be the God and Father of our Lord Jesus Christ! By his great mercy we have been born anew to a living hope through the resurrection of Jesus Christ from the dead." Captain Best recalled, "He reached the hearts of all, finding just the right words to express the spirit of our imprisonment, and the thoughts and resolutions which it had brought." [31]

At the end of the little service, the door was flung open and "two evil-looking men in civilian clothes" came in. They called out Bonhoeffer's name and asked him to follow them. For the prisoners this had come to mean only one thing, a verdict of condemnation and execution. Bonhoeffer bade everyone farewell and, drawing Captain Best aside, gave him a final message to his English friend, Bishop Bell of Chicester. "This is the end but for me also the beginning of life." [32] These were his last recorded words.

The only account of his death has been given by the prison doctor who wrote that, after the verdicts had been read out to Bonhoeffer and those to be hanged with him, he saw "Pastor Bonhoeffer, before taking off his prison garb, kneeling on the floor praying fervently to his God. I was most deeply moved by the way this lovable man prayed, so devout and so certain that God heard his prayer." He added: "At the place of execution, he again said a short prayer and then climbed the steps to the gallows, brave and composed . . . . In the almost 50 years that I worked as a doctor, I have hardly ever seen a man die so entirely submissive to the will of God." [33]

The commemorative tablet erected in the church at Flossenburg, the village where Bonhoeffer was hanged by the S.S., reads very simply: "Dietrich Bonhoeffer: A witness to Jesus Christ among his brothers." To be a witness to Jesus Christ is the principal challenge that the life and death of Bonhoeffer address to all who call themselves disciples of Christ. It is likewise the surest path to that true freedom which enabled Bonhoeffer to see in his own death "the beginning of life." If the theology of

Bonhoeffer can have an uplifting effect on people, it is due to the strongly experienced sense of freedom and zeal for justice that his life and writings have been able to evoke.

In the chapters that follow we will examine in detail the way in which Bonhoeffer's witness was deeply embedded in his love of Christ, in his service of the Christian community, and in his life of faith and prayer. These in turn will be seen as the Christocentric dimensions of the faith that is liberating, not only for peoples captive to an oppressive state, but also for churches called, like Christ, to free people from their bondage to that inner selfishness at the root of all oppression.

2

Christ, the Center of Liberated Life

People who have been electrified by the challenges in Dietrich Bonhoeffer's prison letters are sometimes surprised when researchers inform them of the many sources and influences behind that prison theology. Names like Martin Luther, Friedrich Hegel, Søren Kierkegaard, Friedrich Nietzsche, Ludwig Feuerbach, Wilhelm Dilthey, and Karl Barth make these sources read like a *Who's Who?* of 19th- and 20th-century philosophy and theology and render interpretations of his thought by nonspecialists as varied as reactions to a Rorschach test.[1] Bonhoeffer was indeed as much an eclectic as he was a creative, provocative thinker. Furthermore, his deeds kept apace—and often ahead— of his developing insight into how ecclesial-historical tensions were related to a committed faith and should have been related to both theology and church ministry. However one attempts to structure his theology, though, it is evident that he constantly turns his attention to the robust Christocentrism that informs his understanding not only of the entire theological enterprise but of his life as well.

In his earliest writings Bonhoeffer conceived of theology as directed toward discerning the real presence of Jesus Christ within the community of believers gathered in Jesus' name. This

Christocentric focus would become a major force in his later urging the churches to include the humanitarian cause of peace and even the course of history in their ministries and not be hemmed in by a narrow ecclesialism. He admitted that his thinking on the centrality of Christ tended to become circular, beginning from God's revelation in Christ and terminating in the affirmation that all history and reality are structured by Christ's presence.[2] For him, Christ was the means whereby God is made known to us; God in Christ is the only God Christians can know. He once stated that the "Christian religion stands or falls by belief in divine revelation that became real, tangible, and visible in history."[3] He then identified this tangibility and visibility primarily with the person of Jesus Christ, who manifested God, not in some abstract teaching apart from his humanity, but in the earthly, historical quality of that humanity. Bonhoeffer's attitude in this regard can rightly be called an all-pervading incarnationalism. The significance of Christ's personhood would become the backbone of Bonhoeffer's hope for solutions to the problems besetting both his ministry and his country.

The early Christology of the Berlin dissertations

In working out the foundations of his theological and pastoral ministry, Bonhoeffer brought the "givenness" of Jesus Christ to bear upon the whole process of God's manifestation within a congregation or believing community. His doctoral dissertation, *Sanctorum Communio*, was an ambitious project designed to further his understanding of the relationship of dogma to sociology and social philosophy but more on the ground of what constitutes genuine Christian faith and community, and not on the more empirical basis suggested by the authors he uses.[4]

What is important about *Sanctorum Communio* is the theology of sociality under which Bonhoeffer subsumed his phenomenology of person, community, and his interpretation of the gospel itself.[5] In a later section I will examine the implications of this sociality for ecclesiology and faith. As regards Christology, sociality is involved in Bonhoeffer's portrayal of Jesus' incarnate oneness with humanity which dominates his description of how the form of Christ assumes concrete dimensions in the Christian congregation and, indeed, in the world itself. Bonhoeffer applied the concept of Christ's "corporate personality" as a model to explain the faith-structured nature of social communities and human relationships, even humanity itself. If "Adam" represents created, sinning humanity, Christ is regarded as the "collective person" (*Kollektivperson*) of the "new humanity." In him, our human potential to achieve the perfection or compassion of one created in God's image has become incarnately real. Either "in Adam" or "in Christ" humanity stands as an "I" before the "Thou" of God. This was Bonhoeffer's theological description, not merely of the "social spirit" of human communities, but also of the role of Christ in God's full revelatory communion with his people. Christ makes this communion possible.

To emphasize Christ's central role in restoring the intercommunion of all peoples with his father-God, Bonhoeffer drew a contrast between the "primal state" of an "original unbroken community" and the disrupted community, which sin had caused to turn in on itself. To sin is to act as "Adam," to yield to egocentricity and to close oneself off from the love of others.[6] In the wake of "Adam's sin"—which Bonhoeffer saw repeated in individual sin—individuals and communities became subjected to self-seeking and exploitation. Christ stands in the midst of this otherwise ugly tableau as the "Second Adam," able to bring people close again to God and to each other in a revelatory-reconciling relationship. Christ embodies and actualizes a "new humanity," at one with itself and with his Father.[7] Reconciliation is the third state in the progress of humanity after creation and fall. Christ's person and word became not only Bonhoeffer's societal foundations for community, they were also the essential structure of humanity and the very center of history.

Bonhoeffer accentuated Christ's central relationship to every human community capable of living in mutual love, albeit in a mode imperceptible to most people, through his theological construct of *Stellvertretung*. This word, which nearly defies exact translation,[8] means Christ's vicarious self-giving as representative, deputy, or substitute, making possible the "new humanity" of those renewed through faith and thus reconciled to God, to themselves, and to each other. In short, it is God's love extended in Christ, which most clearly reveals his concern to bring people out of their self-centered isolation into a community of mutual and loving concern. Jesus died in loneliness so that people might know of the depths of that utter loneliness which ensues on the world's sinful self-seeking. "The crucified and resurrected Christ," he wrote, "is recognized by the community as God's incarnate love for people, as his will for renewing the covenant, for establishing his divine lordship and thus for community." [9] Because of Christ's love people can again experience their own lovableness and realize that a genuine Christian existence is "complete self-giving on behalf of others." God's purpose in all this is his desire for the kind of community with his people that his son has personified and initiated. "God's love wants community." [10] Jesus represents that true sociality, so that Bonhoeffer could call the church "Christ existing as community." [11]

Bonhoeffer's second Berlin dissertation, *Act and Being*, written to secure a teaching position at the university, probed more deeply into the anthropological issues at the roots of *Sanctorum Communio* and of his entire Christology. In particular, Bonhoeffer focused on the question of the powerful and power-seeking, dominant and domineering self become increasingly turned inwards in egocentric isolation.[12]

His solution to this problem lay in Christ's powerful personality drawing people to affirm their "better selves" within the Christian community. "Only in the context of a community of persons grounded in and encountered by the self-revealing

Christ can a person be freed from his autonomous, isolated, knowing 'I' which violates reality by understanding everything from itself." [13] The issue he raised in this study was the way genuine freedom brings about oneness between a person's inner self and his or her deeds, between one's being and one's actions. He argued that we find this freedom embodied in Christ. To be truly free, therefore, is to experience an inner unity with Christ and with oneself, in essence, liberation from a tendency to turn one's heart selfishly inward, the "heart turned in on itself," against which Martin Luther had warned.[14] A person's primary liberation, then, is from himself or herself. This means that Christians must live to be caring of others after the model of Christ— in short, that they be wholly directed to Christ.

Bonhoeffer considered this liberation at heart as an appropriation of Christ's own attitude within the "locus" where Christ exists as community. "Here Christ has come the very nearest to humanity," he wrote. "Here he has given himself to humanity. Here he has given himself to his new humanity so that his person embraces in itself all whom he has won ... binding and committing himself to them and they to him." [15] This portrayal of Christ and community lead Bonhoeffer to affirm that Christ frees us by promoting the most intense awareness that freedom itself is always in relationship with others and may entail at any time a sacrifice of oneself. Christ has bound himself to people and inspired their love for and commitment to him and each other in return. The essence of God's freedom in revelation was never more clearly stated than in Bonhoeffer's claim, in opposition to Karl Barth, that God is not free *from* us, protecting his divinity, so to speak. This would be too formal and abstract. Rather, God is "free *for* man. Christ is the Word of his freedom. God is there, which is to say, not in eternal non-objectivity but ... 'haveable,' graspable in his Word within the Church." [16]

It follows from this that Bonhoeffer wanted people to recognize in Christ's humanity and social concern the insight that their own freedom will thrive only insofar as they can be free *for* each other and their communities. This is, likewise, how they will encounter Christ present in their brothers and sisters. Christ reveals the personal character of others to the point that "they themselves become Christ for us in demand and promise." [17] For Bonhoeffer, to be in Christ is to live as brother and sister in the believing community in which Christ is present. Outside this Christ-centered relatedness no liberation is possible. Christ's existence so totally given for us is both the condition of Christian community and the guarantee that this community offers hope for liberation from one's egocentrism.

Christ the center

The other-centered attitude of Christ became also a major theme in Bonhoeffer's Christology lectures delivered at the University of Berlin in the summer semester of 1933. Published in English as *Christ the Center*, these lectures constitute a major attempt by Bonhoeffer during his early teaching career to discern the concrete presence of Jesus Christ within the world without slipping into the theological mire of speculative analyses into *how* the incarnation was possible, into the makeup of the Trinity, or into the exact demarcation between divine and human in Jesus. Points of departure like these, Bonhoeffer declared to his students, would either die the death of abstraction or meander into the dead end of those dull doctrinal formulations so ideal for avoiding a confrontation with the disturbing challenge of Jesus' life. Instead of asking *how* one is able to think out the distinctiveness of the natures in the one person, Bonhoeffer posed to his students what he felt to be the more relevant question: "*Who* is this man of whom it is testified that he is God? " [18]

This, according to Bonhoeffer, was the more meaningful approach of one who is honestly searching for the full implications of Christ's life and death in the world.[19] It would lead, moreover, to the discovery that Christ is the one whose life's energies were devoted to a service of reconciling people to each other and to his Father. Bonhoeffer refused, therefore, to take for a beginning point in Christology any abstract conceptualization of incarnation. If Chalcedon could set the limits of Christological discourse by affirming the two natures, this did not mean that Christians should be forever locked into mere repetition of the incarnation formula or into the further reification that lurks behind every formalized approach to the person of Christ. Chalcedon "stated the *a priori* impossibility and impermissibility of taking the divinity and humanity in Jesus Christ side by side or together or as a relationship of objectifiable entities." [20] To avoid this "objectification" Bonhoeffer proposed that we attempt to understand Christ through patterns of personal relationship.

Such an approach is possible for reasons that become, in turn, the two principal statements in Bonhoeffer's Christology. He insisted, first of all, that, because of his death for sinners and resurrection to life, Jesus is able to relate to people in any era. His presence to the world assumes both temporal and spatial dimensions in the here and now of Christian community life. Through this community his life reaches out to the world.[21] Secondly, Christ's revelatory presence to community must be *personal* if it is truly to be an encounter in love and not a mere power play on Christ's part. Power is but one of the manifold aspects of Christ's presence; one must affirm the wholeness of Christ's person for any assertions about one's being related to Christ to make sense.

Any predication of either divine or human attributes to Christ, therefore, has to be of the whole person: Jesus is fully man and fully God. The questions of how the man Jesus, so limited by time and space, can be contemporaneous and how God can enter time were considered by Bonhoeffer to be beyond human ken and, as a result, meaningless. The only meaningful question for him was: "Who is present and contemporaneous with us here? " [22] To which he answered: "The one person of the God-man Jesus Christ. I do not know who this man Jesus Christ is unless I say at the same time, 'Jesus Christ is God,' and I do not know who the God Jesus Christ is unless I say at the same time, 'Jesus Christ is man'.... God in timeless eternity is not God, Jesus limited by time is not Jesus. Rather God is God in the man Jesus." [23] The dimensions, then, of God's revealing presence pivot upon the givenness of the God-man, present in time and space as man and forever present as God.

Although Bonhoeffer wrote at length of a revelation in presence, he added that God's manifest action in the proclamation of the incarnation must also involve a certain hiddenness by reason of the *skandalon* of his humiliation. This humiliation, which began with the free acceptance of his humanity with all its sinful condition, culminated in Christ's sacrificial death for humankind. Christ is proclaimed as the risen and glorified Lord, but only in the condition of his humiliation as human for the sake of those who are brother and sister unto him. These two aspects cannot be separated. Consequently, when Bonhoeffer described Christ as manifesting God, he reaffirmed God's paradoxical, puzzling revelation in weakness and glorification in humility. This means that one never knows God fully yet one indeed does know God, but only through God's freely initiated, personal relationship with his people in Christ. "Christ is Christ, not as Christ in himself, but in his relation to me. His being Christ is his being *pro me*." [24] By adding the note of hiddenness to this relational aspect of God's revelation, Bonhoeffer hoped to shore up a sense of God's transcendence even in the most immanent activity of his drawing near to us in Christ.

Bonhoeffer, therefore, thought of Christ only in terms of personal relationship, as the Christ who exists *for us* in community. In this, both the *actio Dei* (action on our behalf) and the *praesentia Dei* (being for us) are combined. God has bound himself to us in Christ in the full freedom of his existence, not as *having* the power to exist for us but as *being* that power.[25] God's revelation in Christ is derived from the fact that Christ's whole existence is oriented toward relationship with others. According to Bonhoeffer, this relationship comported three consequences: (1) Christ exists *pro nobis* (for us). This structure is related to Christ's continued historicity among us since Jesus lives for us as "head and firstborn" among his brothers and sisters; (2) Jesus exists to be the Christ for all peoples by acting as our *Stellvertreter* or representative before God. He is the heart and soul of the Christian community; (3) Because of his representative role, he is in the "new humanity," and the fullness of human potential lies, in a way, in him. To experience one's identity with Christ in this communion is at the same time to experience God's graciousness extended to this "new humanity" because of our identity with Christ.[26]

Bonhoeffer further specified that the *pro nobis* structure of Christ's presence is tridimensional: Christ is present in his church as Word, as sacrament, and as community. As Word, Christ encounters people in the communication when truth becomes "an event between two persons . . . ," something that happens "only in community." [27] This Word is both the preached Word and the encounter between persons, who comprise the Christian's sphere of responsibility. Here again, Bonhoeffer chose to stress the concrete, historical context of God's revelatory relationship. Christ is that "other" who challenges us by his Word and who leads us to recognize his presence in our brothers and sisters. This mode of presence is an encounter with transcendent otherness made possible by Jesus' own embodiment of and call to other-centeredness in his existence for us. Bonhoeffer thus subsumed the question of transcendence and existence under the more important personal "question about love for one's neighbor." [28]

Christ's modes of presence as sacrament and as community further explicate his role as mediator of personal relationships, of nature, and even of history. Christ's sacramental presence points up the potential of humanity and, indeed, of nature itself to symbolize the experience of "newness" in one's being freed

from rugged, isolated individualism. Awareness of one's solidarity with Christ can only reinforce the certainty that people
are loved by their fellow believers and called thereby to affirm
their bodily communion with nature, with all peoples, and with
Christ himself who "is the restored creation of our spiritual and
bodily existence." [29] In short, revelation of what Christ's humanity and mediatorship mean for people takes somatic form
in the reality of Christian community. Here Christ is not solely
the Lord but also the Word of God's love, at once divine and
human, personal and social.

The commanding Christ

In the 1930s the German churches were thrust into an ecclesial and political conflict for which their theology was ill-
prepared. Their timidity with regard to the Jewish question, to
threats of disenfranchisement by the state, and their fears of
losing clerical privileges led many church leaders to compromise with their consciences. They justified this in part by the
"traditional" Lutheran doctrine of separation of the two kingdoms (church and state) or by the more self-righteous grounds
of justification by faith alone, rather than works—especially
works which might jeopardize church strength vis-a-vis a might-
ier state. The situation begged for commitment, yet all too few
church leaders knew where to take their stand.

The "meekness" of the churches in the face of state efforts to
co-opt their ministry drove Bonhoeffer to disillusionment with
his own church and to a self-imposed exile. Neither his church
nor his country seemed to have the insight and will to dissent.
In Bonhoeffer's personal life, on the other hand, the word of
Christ's Sermon on the Mount had provided the liberation he
needed to align himself among opponents of Nazification within
the church. Too many ministers lacked such freedom, because,
in his opinion, they had lost touch with the source of all church
strength: unflinching fidelity to the gospel. In effect, the church

had dissipated the courageous voice and powerful freedom of Christ himself.

The Sermon on the Mount had particular appeal for Bonhoeffer in this time because of the uncompromising demands Christ made on those who would be his disciples: an utterly self-sacrificing devotion to the overriding "law" of love in all divine-human relationships. This was something desperately needed in the ecclesial-political crisis churned up by Nazism. Bonhoeffer portrayed the Christ of "costly discipleship" as not merely the mediator of human relationships within community and as the center of history, concepts stressed in earlier works and certainly present as subthemes of his theology of discipleship, but especially as the dominant figure who challenges people to be truly free.

Not that other church people, even among leaders of the Reich church, were not as anxious as Bonhoeffer to be "free" to be "good Christians." According to Bonhoeffer, those who had "nazified" the church simply could not understand the real nature of freedom, because they had separated themselves from that attitude of Jesus, exemplified in the stark cadences of his Sermon on the Mount. True freedom had nothing to do with political blessings on a church or with heavy doses of nationalistic pride. Freedom becomes reality only when joined dialectically to the obedience that asks "what Jesus Christ himself wants of us." [30]

Indeed, the first theme of Bonhoeffer's book *The Cost of Discipleship* stresses that grace is costly because it is the call to follow Christ totally. "It is costly because it cost the life of his Son. . . . Costly grace is the incarnation of God." Cheap grace, on the contrary, is "grace without the cross, grace without Jesus Christ, living and incarnate." [31]

Such a statement reflects Bonhoeffer's continual concern to discern the concrete mode of Jesus' presence as his personal history unfolds into every present. In the period of heightened church crisis, he perceived Christ as the one who invites people to "costly discipleship." Christ can do this because he continues to embody the life of a "new humanity" and to point out the way to true freedom in all its personal and social dimensions.

This call to discipleship is a unique experience of both liberating grace and Christ's command, devoid of legalism, yet binding. "It is," Bonhoeffer observed, "nothing else than bondage to Jesus Christ alone, completely breaking through every program, every ideal, every set of laws." [32] Discipleship then, is a complete attachment to Christ's person. One must be wholly directed to Christ, looking neither to law nor to personal piety nor to the world for fulfillment. The following of Christ exacts a single-mindedness in which one's heart and ambitions are set on Christ alone.[33] Bonhoeffer reminded Christians of Jesus' insistence that no one can serve two masters. It is not a question of a hesitant pondering over where to place one's allegiance. The gospel is clear: one must be decisive in opting for discipleship; one must face up to the demands of the Sermon on the Mount. Those who waver or hide behind the totems of society probably "are unwilling to stand alone before Jesus and to be compelled to decide with their eyes fixed on him alone." [34] Other attractions are but mirages of the light of life, which emanates from Christ.

The deeper issue in Bonhoeffer's raw injunction against dividing one's loyalties is the question of Christ's mediating role in Christian life. Christ is the center of all things, standing between God and his people, leading people to love each other. Hence there can be no "immediacy" in the way we are to relate to the world. The false gods of power, ambition, and pleasure offer such an untroubled and uncritical "direct access" to themselves. Those who live in Christ must accept, rather, that the whole world was created through and in him. Christ is sole mediator of reality.[35] Every relationship must, therefore, be refracted through the presence of Christ, who personifies the "new humanity" and the "new creation."

It is not difficult to read between the lines of Bonhoeffer's argument here to see shredded the claims of Nazism to mediate one's relationship with God through the "cornerstones of racial purity and national pride." The Nazi seduction of Christianity had lulled church leaders and their people into thinking they had been "freed" for "direct relationship" with every aspect of the "world" (read "Nazism") with a good conscience. Bonhoeffer took aim at those who ignore the cross of judgment on every human pretension to a "clean conscience" in his ironic statement: "Jesus has reconciled us to God; we can then, it is supposed, return to the world and enjoy our direct relation with it with a good conscience—although that world is the very world which crucified Christ! This is to equate the love of God with the love of the world." [36] The Christian, on the contrary, must be a lover of Christ and his cross in order to enter fully into the rhythms of Jesus' own salvific death and resurrection. Christ's cross is both the test and the destiny of a disciple of Christ.

This cross is also the mark of a genuine Christian community. *The Cost of Discipleship* continued the insights of Bonhoeffer's Berlin dissertations, emphasizing that Christ's communion with humanity and his mediatorship make real the community of disciples who both believe and live by the gospel. Hope in the "new humanity"—when so many people were worshiping Teutonic myths—becomes possible because Christ's death and resurrection overcome the sinful arrogance, self-centeredness and depersonalization of the "old humanity." Disciples can affirm their bond of love in the community that is his bodily presence, because discipleship is never separated from the brotherhood and sisterhood able to share faith and to encourage one another in sufferings for the sake of Christ's Word. As Bonhoeffer observed, "Their goal is to become 'as Christ.' Christ's followers always have his image before their eyes, and in its light all other images are screened from their sight." [37]

Christ, the unity of human existence

In Bonhoeffer's view not only does Christ reveal the nature of true discipleship, but, as mediator of the revelatory relationship between God and his people, Christ has also lived for his brothers and sisters at the very center of what life for God should be. He had, in the words of Paul, "fulfilled the law," that symbol of sin and failure; therefore he was able to point to the possibility of a new existence in the most intimate union with him. History itself must likewise move toward a fulfillment when Christ will be revealed as the hidden center of all history. This had already been implicitly proclaimed in the prophetic hope of Israel. It was accomplished, but in a veiled manner, by God's entering history. This is why Bonhoeffer contended that the meaning of history was mediated at its hidden center by the crucified Christ.[38] Although the world had been reconciled in Christ and in Christ God had spoken his word of justification, this reality had not yet attained the fullness of the end time when Christ would be revealed as God's final reconciliation of all creation. The final Word had been, so to speak, pronounced in the cross of Jesus, but insofar as Christians live in the here and now, between "penultimate and ultimate," they must experience the tension between present faith and the final times, when the hope of universal brotherhood and sisterhood will be realized.

Despite the tension inherent in such living between the existential present and the eschatological future, Bonhoeffer discerned a paradoxical unity in the historical process. This unity he derives from his Christological understanding of all reality, structuring not only the life of faith but the meaning underlying history. From that unique event which was the life of Jesus Christ, Bonhoeffer traced the intelligibility behind all other events of history. In terms of this Christological structure Bonhoeffer also attempted to collate all the penultimate realities of life and dislodge Christianity from its traditional "thinking in two spheres."

In his *Ethics* he explicated and broadened the notion of the centrality of Christ in an even more universal direction. More so than any other modern author, with the possible exception of Teilhard de Chardin, Bonhoeffer wanted to merge Christ and the world into a dialectical unity. His aim was to take all the traditional opposites—natural-supernatural, profane-sacred, rational-revelational—and to show that these concepts have an original unity in Christ. He was as equally opposed to separating these concepts as he was to imposing pseudo-unity on them by forcing them into some inflated sacred system. According to Bonhoeffer, all of reality, whether it be considered specifically sacred or profane, had been taken up by God in Christ from the outset of creation. To split off the profane from the sacred, the natural from the supernatural, and to assign them an autonomous sphere apart from God would miss the point that these so-called spheres have their reality only in the reality of God. "The whole reality of the world is already drawn into Christ and bound together in him, and the movement of history consists solely in divergence and convergence in relation to this center." [39] The unity of reality would, then, derive from Christ and, on the part of human attitudes, from faith in Christ.

The brunt of Bonhoeffer's criticism of those who separate secular reality from the reality of Christ was directed against the effects of maintaining such a dichotomy. Inevitably this had led to an attitude of perpetual conflict, a segmented Christianity unresponsive to the world's needs. A unity was needed, yet not a unity that would simply identify the worldly with the Christian. The Christian and secular elements of life share reality and are united in the reality of Christ, so that neither can assume a static independence in relation to the other. They stand in a polemical unity. Christianity can never withdraw from the world, but neither can the world isolate itself from the fellowship revealed in Jesus Christ. Bonhoeffer declared further that Christ constitutes the origin, the essence, and the goal of all reality, a position somewhat reminiscent of Teilhard de Chardin's Christogenesis.[40]

Bonhoeffer was here promoting an incarnationalism in which knowledge of Christ is linked to the proper knowledge of history and reality. He claimed that this is possible not only from the revelation of how Christ structures reality but also from a consideration of concrete human situations experienced by Christ. Christ was not alien to our history, but on the contrary, "It is he who alone has borne and experienced the essence of the real in his own body, who has spoken from the standpoint of reality as no man on earth can do, who alone has fallen victim to no ideology, but who is the truly real one, who has borne within himself and fulfilled the essence of history, and in whom the law of the life of history is embodied." [41] This Christocentric perspective was determinative for Bonhoeffer of the Christian orientation toward life. By taking Christ as a point of departure for a specific Christian commitment, he steered clear of abstract principles and pious generalities unrelated to the lived reality. History, as fulfilled in Christ, thus became for Bonhoeffer the area where people exercise their freedom for responsible action.

Jesus, the man for others

Bonhoeffer's letters and papers from prison reflect his struggle to discern the specific way Christ is manifest in a world torn apart by war and hatred. "What is bothering me incessantly," he wrote to Bethge, "is the question . . . who Christ really is for us today." [42] In prison he called for an even more practical search into the concrete form Christ was assuming in the critical time during and beyond the war, as well as the appropriate response to this Christic manifestation. The description of this contemporary revelation of God in Christ that can be derived from the letters exhibits many of the characteristics observed in the Christology lectures of 1933 and may, therefore, be related to the basic affirmation that God exists for us in Jesus Christ.

If, in Bonhoeffer's Christology lectures, the theme of God's suffering in Christ appeared in the dialectic with the meaning of resurrection,[43] in his prison writings the dialectic seems to slant more one-sidedly to a description of the humiliated Christ, who in his agony and death discloses the extent of God's love for his people.[44] The probable reason for this stronger accentuation of the "theology of the cross" is stated in a letter of June 27, 1944. There he mentioned that the redemption myths had emphasized somewhat disproportionately the other side of death and the liberation to a better world, whereas the crucified Christ proclaimed by the gospel stressed involvement in all the difficulties of the present life.[45] In other words, the Christian must face up to the stark reality of an earthly life in conformity with the crucified Christ.

The text of Mark 15:34, "My God, my God, why hast thou forsaken me?" was presented by Bonhoeffer not only as what such conformity with Christ might entail but also as the touchstone of the life of faith, which has a strong this-worldly dimension. The cry of abandonment from the cross signified to Bonhoeffer that Christ chose to participate fully in the human condition, even to the death exacted for such a total involvement. Not even Christ could avoid the human consequences of sacrificing oneself for the sake of others, immersed in worldly duties, sharing both earthly blessings and sufferings. "Like Christ himself ('My God, my God, why hast thou forsaken me?') he [the Christian] must drink the earthly cup to the dregs, and only in his doing so is the crucified and risen Lord with him, and he crucified and risen with Christ. The world must not be prematurely written off; in this the Old and New Testaments are one." [46]

Bonhoeffer's point was that Christ was not like a *deus ex machina* who came to earth from on high, remained supremely aloof except to intervene at certain moments with opportune miracles, and then departed virtually untouched by the world's inexorable laws. Christ experienced the absence of God at the very moment when he ached for deliverance. Christ was a complete man and thereby able not only to reconcile people to God but also to reveal something of what it means to live as a person before God. Like Christ, people must experience the "absence of God" in order to recognize the authentic God at the center of their lives.

In prison Bonhoeffer criticized those church leaders who in their preaching or catechizing had presented a distorted picture of God as someone set apart in transcendent aloofness. This to him was certainly not the God who had freely bound himself to his people in the person of Jesus Christ. He insisted that God was not revealed so much in the power but in the very weakness of Christ. Christ was related to people in his sufferings, not as the glib answer to problems or as the powerful founder of a religion preying on human weakness. The Christ whom Bonhoeffer proclaimed as the Lord of the world and as present at the center of human life must be understood in the perspective of the cross. Only the suffering Christ could disclose the true depths of God's kinship with his creatures. God was not "beyond," but by his cross he was related to people in the very midst of life. This is the biblical picture of God in Christ, which Bonhoeffer expressed in a new Christological title, "the man for others."

Bonhoeffer's efforts to dismiss the "idols" that philosophical speculation and religiosity had made of divinity led him, in explaining who God is, to concentrate almost exclusively on how God is present in every genuinely human relationship. If the death of Jesus reveals something of the depths of God's love for his people, Jesus as "the man for others" not only extends his Father's compassion for his people in a very palpable, caring way, he also gives an example of the self-transcendence to which every Christian is called. Hence in the "Outline for a Book" Bonhoeffer affirmed that, "our relation to God is not a 'religious' relationship to the highest, most powerful, and best Being imaginable—that is not authentic transcendence—but our relation to God is a new life in 'existence for others,' through participation in the being of Jesus . . . 'the man for others,' and therefore the Crucified, the man who lives out of the transcendent." [47] This is genuine faith in the transcendent God; it is likewise the way faith enables people to transcend every tendency toward ingrown selfishness.

Christ's death on the cross became the supreme expression of his human destiny, marking him forever as a person whose whole purpose in life was to serve others. This distinctive title, "the man for others," with its emphasis on self-sacrificing service, sums up the various aspects that form the figure of Christ emerging from Bonhoeffer's theology. Bonhoeffer could describe Christ as "the man for others" because his basic idea of God in Christ is of one who exists for people in the most total act of his self-giving: the humiliation of the cross. The whole creaturely existence of Christ is oriented to others. In this, God revealed himself as one willing to sacrifice himself for his people, to become a God who suffers.

Accordingly, Bonhoeffer demanded that theological discourse about God begin, not in those "boundary situations" such as sin, failure, suffering, and death, but in the fullness of human life and strength. He felt that descriptions of God's relationship with his creatures had become distorted by a pietistical manipulation of the Scriptures, which had, in effect, dismissed God to the realm of some ethereal beyond, thus preserving God's majestic otherness at the expense of his incarnate nearness.

The paradox of God's transcendent otherness and his free choice to give himself to his people were resolved in Bonhoeffer's prison theology in favor of a "this-worldly" transcendence. He refused to speak of any transcendence that would edge God into the realm of the abstract. Both God's being and his freedom were understood by Bonhoeffer as directed toward his people. God is free *for* us.[48] In this way, the mode of transcendence and freedom manifested through Christ became a model for the ultimate transcendence and freedom to which every person is drawn by God. Because Christ was the man for others, all Christians responding in faith to Christ are called to unselfish service of others and thus to work for the eventual reconciliation of all people in Christ. Bonhoeffer wanted to rediscover the contemporary form of Christ, which, like a *cantus firmus* or underlying theme, could bring all the counterpoints of Christian life into harmony. Jesus Christ directs people not only to the authentic God depicted in the Bible but also to that wholeness of life to which every person aspires. True freedom is to be experienced in the pursuit and attainment of such wholeness.

3

The Liberation
of Faith

On the day after the failure of the July 20 assassination attempt on Hitler's life, Bonhoeffer composed a poem as a birthday present for his friend Eberhard Bethge. This poem, "Stations on the Road to Freedom," which describes the stages of a person's quest for true freedom, is among the most autobiographical of Bonhoeffer's writings. As the stanzas so poignantly note, the struggle for freedom begins in discipline and action but reaches fulfillment only in suffering and death.[1]

In a way Bonhoeffer was reflecting on his own realization that true liberation had to be experienced within the paradoxical context of that obedience unto death demanded by one's commitment to Jesus Christ. If the eagerness to be free could lead Bonhoeffer to *resist* both an unjust state and a weak church, this same desire also brought him to *submit* to the inexorable demands of the gospel and the consequences of his decision to join the conspiracy. As he remarked in the letter of February 21, 1944, it is "impossible to define the boundary between *resistance* and *submission* on abstract principles; but both of them must exist, and both must be practiced. Faith demands this elasticity of behavior. Only so can we stand our ground in each situation as it arises, and turn it to gain."[2] How Bonhoeffer "stood his ground" in the situation of his theological career, church ministry, and political involvement and thereby showed how faith can "liberate" from evil is the theme of this chapter.

Theological anthropology and self-transformation

According to Bonhoeffer, faith is such an integral part of being fully human that not only full self-understanding and freedom, but theological reflection as well, are impossible without it. "The basis of all theology," he wrote, "is the fact of faith. Only in the act of faith as a *direct act* is God recognized as the reality which is beyond and outside our thinking, of our whole existence." [3] Early in his theological career Bonhoeffer was convinced that faith alone could unravel the network of divine-human relationships that constitute the Christian community and humanity itself. All of the categorical structures of revelation, such as one's "being in Christ" or "being in the Christian community" were intelligible only when primed by the faith whereby God places people in a special situation of responsibility. Faith, as a contingent act of God, had to be present at every stage of revelation and personal growth.[4] In Bonhoeffer's theology, revelation can never be considered complete until God brings people to a certain degree of explicit consciousness, enabling them in faith to enter into a personal relationship with God in Christ and to accept the self-transformation this effects.

Bonhoeffer himself experienced such a self-transformation. We know something of this change in his outlook from a letter sent early in 1936 to a girlfriend. Referring to a development prior to 1933, he admitted:

I plunged into work in a very unchristian way. An . . . ambition that many noticed in me made my life difficult. . . . Then something happened, something that has changed and transformed my life to the present day. For the first time I discovered the Bible. . . . I had often preached, I had seen a great deal of the Church, and talked and preached about it—but I had not yet become a Christian. . . . I know that at that time I turned the doctrine of Jesus Christ into something of personal advantage for myself. . . . Also I had never prayed, or prayed only very little. For all my abandonment, I was quite pleased with myself. Then the Bible, and in particular the Sermon on the Mount, freed me from that. Since then everything has changed. . . . It was a great liberation.[5]

Bethge adds in his biographical comment that Bonhoeffer had come in the meantime to dislike his most abstract book, *Act and Being*.[6] However this may be, it is in *Act and Being* and the earlier dissertation, *Sanctorum Communio*, and other works of the 1930s, that we are able to perceive more clearly the inner turmoil Bonhoeffer was going through at the time, a struggle hidden from all but a few intimate friends. We have touched on those problems in the preceding chapter in connection with the manner in which he looked to the life and example of Jesus Christ as the personal way to true liberation. Here we will examine how Bonhoeffer's self-understanding disposed him to a deeper awareness of his need to commit himself totally to gospel values embodied in the person of Jesus.

Act and Being is a labyrinth of intersecting analyses of how sociality is related to revelation, how revelation is concretized in church, and how a Christocentric epistemology must inspirit the ontology of one's "being in Christ." But the central focus— and, therefore, the clue to what Bonhoeffer intends to achieve through his thesis—is theological anthropology.[7] Bonhoeffer stated in his preface to *Act and Being* that he wished to reconcile the dialectic of genuine transcendental ("act") and ontological ("being") approaches to the reality of revelation within the social category of church understood as a "being in Christ."

This stated aim can be misleading.[8] The real issue is how the human person is freed from servitude to self and led to a revelatory relationship with God in Jesus Christ. True autonomy, Bonhoeffer pointed out, becomes a possibility only when an individual is saved from his egocentric individualism and made aware of his responsibilities within the ecclesial-human community. Here it is a question of how God moves the knowing subject to trust in him as he is revealed in his Son, Jesus Christ, and of how the ensuing relationship cannot be adequately described through static categories of being. Nor can the relationship be atomized or reduced to only those occasions when God's actions are most clearly perceived and celebrated.

Bonhoeffer first analyzed how the autonomous person attempts to understand himself solely from within his own intellectual powers, only to contend that such an effort eventually comes to grief in narcissistic isolation. The only valid premise for true self-understanding is God's revelation in Christ. This revelation is, in turn, anchored within the Christian community, where one overcomes alienation and experiences liberation by accepting responsibility for others.

Throughout the critical sections of this book Bonhoeffer tried to pick apart those philosophies that fed human pretensions with claims of "autonomous self-understanding." He saw lurking in this rugged quest for individualistic autonomy the attitude that places the human person rather than God at the root of growth to Christian maturity, and the inveterate tendency to reduce reality to the thinking "I." In such a reason-centered constellation even God appears to be harnessed to human consciousness and made to bless still another badly camouflaged human attempt at self-justification. "What offends Christian thought in any autonomous self-understanding is that it considers man capable of bestowing truth on himself. . . . Thought is as little able as good works to deliver the *cor curvum in se* (heart turned in on itself) from itself." [9]

Bonhoeffer's main concern here was soteriological: how Christ overcomes the alienation from God, others, and the self that ensues whenever one becomes imprisoned in the circle of isolated individualism.[10] "Whoever countenances the idea that he need only arrive at himself to be in God is doomed to hideous disillusion in experiencing the utter introversion, the treadmill confinement to the self, of the very loneliest solitude, with its tormenting desolation and sterility." [11]

This picture is bleak. It is also a strong personal statement of Bonhoeffer's deepest fears about his own faith. When he cautioned against narcissistic introspection, he was working out within himself a power struggle between the pull of his own self-serving academic ambitions and the attractive, more powerful personality of Jesus Christ. He criticized philosophical systems in terms of their over-confidence in the powers of the human intellect to explain reality. At the same time, he acknowledged the need for a "pure" transcendentalism, which can resist being dominated by the thinking-knowing subject and thereby become an important factor in genuine faith. The act of faith, whereby one is directed to Christ who evades being drawn into the orbit of the domineering ego, is fundamentally a relationship with the transcendent God.

Bonhoeffer still wondered, however, whether one could long resist the temptation to reduce all transcendence to one's own inner subjectivity.[12] He fashioned correctives for this tendency from human sociality. If traditional ontology, or the emphasis on "being" as prior to action, defends the priority of God who alone can attract people into a faith relationship, ontology seen as social reality preserves a sense of continuity in one's faith against actualistic notions which stress faith's episodic character in peak moments of grace and decisions to obey God. The fact that people are drawn into church communities or congregations bespeaks continuity in one's faith. One's church offers opportunities to show a concern for others which, in turn, helps snap people out of their selfishness. True transcendentalism stresses God's *freedom*; ontology, God's *priority* and *steadfastness*. Faith is neither a once-for-all possession nor an opportunity to use God as one might manipulate other people when only the reality of the self exists. God is free *from* all those human efforts that make him an object to be manipulated.

Yet the essence of God's freedom, as we know it from the scriptural testimony, lies in his will to exist *for* his creatures.[13] Such is God's nature. Such, too, the calling of every man and woman to experience freedom in self-sacrificing service of others. Hence, Bonhoeffer insisted that this aspect of freedom is intertwined with God's revelation, which can occur only in community.[14] "God reveals himself in the church as person. The community is God's final revelation of himself as Christ existing as community." [15] God has brought himself into this community in the person of Christ, and there he reveals his own other-centeredness. This serves as a model for that authentic freedom whereby people "in Christ can find their true humanity in being free for another and for their communities." [16] The "being" of revelation is the community to which God has bound himself in personal communion with his children. Bonhoeffer used this social category to affirm that the Christian community transcends each individual believer because of the continuity in faith which it promotes. This continuity is not to be found in a powerfully structured institution, nor in absolute, unchanging doctrines, nor even in the possession of an inerrant Bible. It lies, rather, in that gathering of honest, loving believers who relate to each other in Christ.

In Bonhoeffer's perspective Christ encounters people "from without" their own subjectivity and is not manipulable either by individuals or by religion itself. This is so because of the nature of justification, which people cannot attain on their own. What is more, the encounter with God in Christ and in one's community takes place at that level where the "other" must be allowed freedom to relate in true personhood without danger of being reduced to one's own self-image or imperialistic ambitions. It is because of the personal character of Christ's existence in community that others can make those demands on one's person and time that are ultimately at the foundations of true liberation. "It is only from the person of Christ," Bonhoeffer contended, "that other persons acquire for man the character of personhood. In this way they themselves become Christ for us in demand and promise, in their existential impositions upon us from without. At the same time they become, as such, the pledge of revelation's continuity." [17]

From this passage it is clear that Bonhoeffer viewed the presence of others in community as a mode of Christ's own liberating presence. Others never exist only in the abstract, and it would be a travesty of true community for a person to claim to love humanity but to have no loved ones. In fact, Bonhoeffer insisted that one's life in community is either an existence "in Adam" or "in Christ"; either one stands alone "in untruth," through treating people as objects to be used—or one lives "in truth," through breaking out of the solitude of self-glorification and excessive self-love.[18]

Through his personal-communitarian emphasis Bonhoeffer envisaged faith as epitomized in the person of Jesus Christ, who cannot be reduced to the believing subject and who brings people into a revelatory relationship with God and others. Christ is knowable personally as an "objective" concrete manifestation of God. Yet, precisely because he is free, he refuses to be brought within the dominating power of the knowing "I":

> In the act of belief, which Christ himself creates within me, inasmuch as he gives me the Holy Spirit who hears and believes within me, he also proves himself the free Lord of my existence. Christ "is" only "in" faith, yet he is master of my faith. He is the absolute extrinsicality for my existence, but for that very reason he impinges on it, gives himself to be known by it.[19]

Faith involves knowledge that one is in relationship with Christ, who gives himself to a believer through the members of the community. This is the same Christ who exercises power over believers as he creates within them the faith that justifies.

That this faith is not controlled by human reflection is an important facet of Bonhoeffer's early theology. As he wrote in a letter to his brother-in-law, he feared "running only into a divine counterpart" of himself.[20] He portrayed one's directedness toward Christ, therefore, as an act in which Christ is personally encountered in people within the community. Faith had to be a *direct* act (*actus directus*) about which reflection (*actus reflexus*) could neither produce a fully intelligible analysis nor exercise any cognitive control. He was critical of efforts to broaden the understanding of faith to include reflection as a necessary element. Reflection on faith, he argued, yields at best only the past spoken word of Christ. When reflection on faith is absolutized or made to seem more important than the relationship with God at the heart of true belief, it leads to religiosity.

Bonhoeffer retreated from asserting the possibility of achieving a full analysis of the act of faith. His reasoning on this point is disarming in its ingenuousness. The answer to the "how?" of faith can come only from recognizing faith's God-givenness, which is indemonstrable. "Faith looks not on itself but on Christ alone. Whether faith *is* faith can be neither ascertained nor even believed, but the faith which believes *is* faith." [21] Bonhoeffer affirmed this because he held equally that people have been placed in the community only by God's salvific-revelatory actions in Christ and that, consequently, in faith we must realize we exert no control over Christ's transforming presence within the community.

The new reality is founded by the personal Word of Christ moving people into the mainstream of truth, which is in the person of Christ himself. This truth is given, revealed, lived; by it, a person is known by God, who redirects one's self-understanding to Christ. If there is any reflection in the act of faith, it can only be in the act of recollection, in which the theologian or preacher can come to some understanding of the self affected by God's Word. But this is itself more a service to the community; it is not justifying faith, which eludes both reflection and a full cognitive grasp.[22]

Bonhoeffer related this faith to one's "new existence" in Christ. Through faith people pass from the condition of "untruth" to that transformation of self whose cognitive realization depends in turn on faith in God's Word.[23] Bonhoeffer maintained that knowledge of one's spiritual growth in faith can itself be derived only from the revelation, which tells of how Christ has shattered one's solitary concentration on self to instill true self-knowledge and an other-centered outlook on life. The death of the narcissistic "I" in living in and for Christ can be brought to explicit awareness not by any intellectual dissection of the act of justification but solely in direct contemplation of Christ.[24]

From this line of reasoning it is evident that Bonhoeffer was trying to avoid handing faith's creative energies over to the domination of the thinking, reflecting "I." A person's true freedom derives from Christ alone. On the believer's part, faith involves essentially a deliberate, grace-initiated turning toward Christ and, secondarily, a recognition of one's sociality with others in Christ. Bonhoeffer feared that people might yield to the temptation of whittling faith down to a cognition in which people progressively discover who God is and who they are in God's designs, without ever integrating the two into a concrete life of faith. Faith, on the contrary, must ultimately retain its Christ-directedness in order to keep its footing within the Christian community and to achieve true liberation of the self.

Freedom for costly discipleship

The liberating dimension in the life of faith, as experienced by Bonhoeffer and incorporated into his theology in the 1930s, is the maturity a person attains in abandoning self-centeredness and in commiting himself wholly to Jesus Christ. In this perspective freedom assumes the proportions of utter devotion to others after the manner of Jesus, whose cross of discipleship reveals the paradoxical nature of true liberation. In *Act and Being* Bonhoeffer described God's freedom as his existence *for* his creatures.[25] Such, too, was the unconditioned freedom that impelled Jesus to be, as Bonhoeffer would express it in his letters from prison, "the man for others." [26] Jesus, the image of God, related to people in a manner that both respected and promoted their autonomy. One acts as a true child of God and brother or sister of Christ in adopting the same altruistic attitude of Christ.

This is why Bonhoeffer later insisted in his lectures on Genesis that freedom is not something a person "has for himself but something he has for others. . . . In truth, freedom is a relationship between two persons. Being free means being free *for* the other, because the other has bound me to him. Only in relationship with the other am I free." [27] Being committed as disciples of Christ to serve others is how Bonhoeffer interpreted the gospel message that as Christians we are bound to the very self-sacrificing freedom of God himself who became "weak" for our sakes. This is what he called living "in the center of life through Christ" and in the light of his resurrection. We thus become "free for God" inasmuch as we are dedicated to those who also may address God as Father and to whom Christ is brother—even though they are not conscious of it.[28]

This kind of freedom presupposes, however, that one is also liberated from the disorderliness that impedes wholehearted commitment to the gospel. Again Bonhoeffer attempted to preserve the paradox of Christian discipleship. The faith of the disciple of Christ is liberating only if joined with obedience to Christ's word. Hence Bonhoeffer's injunction in *The Cost of Discipleship*: "*Only he who believes is obedient, and only he who is obedient believes.*" [29] Bonhoeffer was not arguing that liberating faith needs to be supplemented by some action. Rather, he saw the whole sphere of Christian obedience to God's will in any age inextricably bound to faith and the gospel of what God has done for us in Christ. Faith and obedience are linked together in a dialectical and indissoluble unity, in which willingness to obey and serve God is the natural and spontaneous note of a life governed by dedication to the person and mission of Jesus Christ.[30] Bonhoeffer's close friend Eberhard Bethge once recalled that the pairing of these reciprocal concepts "sounded rather shocking to all of us at the time. There was hardly a German theologian who hadn't left the world of 'simple obedience,' i.e., the world of understanding the Sermon on the Mount literally, to the pietists, the enthusiasts and the radicals. But he tried to win it back for a liberated faith." [31]

At the same time, Bonhoeffer cautioned against giving the "virtuous action" of obedience the stature of condition for faith and against performing an action with the *intention of acquiring faith*. Such he thought to be a blatant attempt to be justified by works, a complete misapprehension of how both faith and justification can come from God alone. In no way did Bonhoeffer wish to diminish God's total initiative in revealing himself and in bringing people to faith. He counseled, instead, fixing one's attention not on the work, but on the "Word of Christ" summoning to belief so that obedience to this Word might itself prove to be an act of faith.

We should keep in mind, though, that the important note for Bonhoeffer was not whether faith or obedience may come first.[32] His supreme concern was the reality to which faith is directed: God's self-disclosure in the person of Jesus Christ. Discipleship means nothing less than living in conformity with Christ as he is revealed within the community and being ready to obey Christ as unconditionally as the first disciples.[33]

The question Bonhoeffer hoped to resolve through a renewed sense of discipleship was how to bring one's self-seeking and self-centeredness under the authority of Jesus Christ and his command in the Sermon on the Mount.[34] Single-minded obedience to Christ was, for Bonhoeffer, the essence of Christian discipleship. *The Cost of Discipleship* is as much a communication of his own shift from the "phraseological to the real" life of a disciple of Christ as it is a challenge to the German church in its struggle against nazism.[35] Christ is the dominant figure the community must follow integrally if it is to be the bearer of

Christ's word and the body of his person encountering individuals and laying claim to their life and service.[36] The community is to be the concrete shape Christ takes in the world.

The failure of the church of the 1930s to be this Christ to the world was due to its having succumbed to the seductive lure of "cheap grace," or what Bonhoeffer called "the justification of sin without the justification of the sinner."[37] This "cheap grace" kept faith solely on the intellectual level and justified the indifference of mediocre Christians who refused to become involved in the problems then besetting church and country. In one of his most chilling judgments Bonhoeffer complained that many of his fellow Christians "have gathered like ravens around the carcass of cheap grace and there have drunk of the poison which has killed the life of following Christ."[38]

One of the most destructive elements of that poison was the worship of power and pursuit of counterfeit discipleship. Would-be disciples could thus dull their consciences through homage to the totems of their own ambitions, such as the power and fame that result from success in proselytizing or the mastery of Christian ideas and principles, the "phraseological" world so familiar to Bonhoeffer. This was an adroit stratagem for avoiding the cost of genuine discipleship, all the while basking in the self-satisfaction of one's own personal success and career advancement.

The theme of "costly grace" was Bonhoeffer's answer to the seduction of counterfeit discipleship. This involves one's whole life, not simply the academic side of Christianity. It also demands, in the acceptance of Christ's cross, a change in one's outlook or a total obedience to the command of Christ, whose power and authority overcome the power of the ambitious, self-serving ego. Disciples who hear and obey the word of Christ's command are not free to pursue a self-styled and self-serving mode of discipleship.[39] On the contrary, they must, like Abraham, break with every trace of self-will in order to be "transformed by Christ."[40] "It is not for us to choose which way we shall follow,"

Bonhoeffer wrote. "That depends on the will of Christ." [41] Often, this obedient following of Christ entails a hidden break with one's past or one's apparent goals of the present and eventually an open commitment to the cross of discipleship. Such was the pattern in Bonhoeffer's own life when he decided to leave the university and a promising career as a theologian in order to become more actively involved in the church struggle.[42]

That decision, with its open avowal of opposition to the Nazi regime, was a major step in Bonhoeffer's own espousal of the cross of discipleship and in his eventual liberation from personal ambitiousness. He had come to realize that the Christ of the Sermon on the Mount was challenging his followers to accept even death itself for the sake of the gospel. "Discipleship means allegiance to the suffering Christ." [43] Refusal of the cross signalled that one had bargained for "cheap grace" and, in effect, had forfeited true fellowship with Christ. Bonhoeffer's conviction about the need to abandon one's attachments to careerism and self-centered ambitions in order to surrender oneself fully to Christ accounts for his vinegary judgments on his own church so firmly ensconced in the pyramid of lies, misplaced patriotism, and timidity that made Hitlerism possible. "When Jesus calls a man," Bonhoeffer declared, "he bids him come and die." [44] In that death for others lay the paradoxical strength of the disciple engaged in radical, uncompromising obedience to Jesus Christ, whose obedience unto death was itself the path to true freedom and life.

For Bonhoeffer, the "cost of discipleship" was one's own life. Death to self-interest, to sin, and to the drive for security is costly. Yet, if one's life is to be patterned after the example of Jesus Christ, it is the only way for the disciple to share fully in Christ's ministry of forgiveness and in the fellowship of Christian faith. Such is the power of Christ that even the apparent weakness of human suffering can be turned to the advantage of the gospel, and the reconciliation of people in love and freedom is made a possibility.

Faith, freedom, and responsibility

The shape of Bonhoeffer's life and, consequently, his theology was formed in the kiln of Nazi political and ecclesiastical policy. His reflection on the history of his time and on the proper reaction of a Christian community to the vulgar, if not downright brutal, attempts of the Nazi regime to manipulate the churches was hasty and more the thinking of a committed believer than a systematic analysis of the historical situation. If theologian and pastor Bonhoeffer could hardly be called a political analyst, he nonetheless had remarkably cogent views on how a state should function with regard to freedom for both individuals and community. His reading of the importance of specific events in the context of their far greater ramifications was accurate to the point of being creative, especially as regards the "Jewish Question," Hitler's threat to basic human rights, the issue of war and peace, and the nature of the ecumenical movement.

Because of Bonhoeffer's ability to interpret specific historical events in the light of their importance for Christian faith, his sharp judgment in *The Cost of Discipleship* against reliance on human strength alone was further refined in the war years. In *The Cost of Discipleship* he correctly indicted that self-serving tendency to dominate others and to set the self up in either witting or unwitting opposition to the Christian gospel. What is not so clear from Bonhoeffer's caution against the aberrations of ambitiousness and the misuse of power is the difference between pursuit of power to dominate and manipulate others and the development of that mature ego strength needed in order to overcome evil and to suffer with Christ at the hands of the godless.[45]

Left unqualified, Bonhoeffer's writings of the "Cost of Discipleship" era could give the impression that, having given oneself over to the strength and command of Jesus Christ, one's "weakness can be indiscriminately affirmed." [46] This leads to a certain ambivalence in Bonhoeffer's theology of discipleship. Bonhoeffer appears to vacillate between a discipleship based on surrender to the dominating power of Jesus Christ and stress on the acceptance of suffering 'and weakness in imitation of the crucified Christ. Clifford Green has perceptively noted: "Corresponding to this ambivalence, the anthropology vacillates between, on the one hand, a combative power in the disciples and a downright weakness which Christians must learn to accept, and, on the other hand, a strength in Christian action and suffering whose source is the Christ of the *theologia crucis.*" [47]

Although the affirmation of God's paradoxical strength in weakness is present as a subtheme in *The Cost of Discipleship*, it is not yet that more mature appreciation of faith's inherent relatedness to human autonomy and freedom of the resistance years. When Bonhoeffer's understanding of faith dictated not only that a person accept God's command but also that he act to shape history, a more dialectical appraisal of power prevailed. The counsel that a true disciple of Christ must yield to the powerful command of his Lord had about it a certain quietistic acknowledgment that the events of history and the provision of material needs were in the control of God; people were themselves unable "to alter the circumstances of this world. Only God can take care," Bonhoeffer then wrote, "for it is he who rules the world. Since we *cannot* take care, since we are so completely powerless, we *ought* not to do it either. If we do, we are dethroning God and presuming to rule the world ourselves." [48]

This assertion is remote from Bonhoeffer's insistence in his *Ethics* that Christians have the responsibility to do their utmost to promote gospel values in the singular events of history. To accept the status quo, particularly when the necessities of life were denied and human rights violated, was considered by Bonhoeffer an infidelity to the gospel. The person of faith must somehow, under the guidance of the gospel and according to the basic human values and rights proclaimed by Christ, assume responsibility for turning history in the proper direction. Bonhoeffer was convinced that ecclesiastical quietism or retreat into a "let-God-handle-it" attitude in the era of Nazi oppression would be tantamount to an irresponsible surrender to the forces of evil and a self-serving escape from the cross of discipleship. History had to be shaped by the Christian, and this meant that faith had to be inspired by a desire for freedom and a sense of responsibility.

In this connection, Bonhoeffer's correct diagnosis of the importance of the "Jewish Question" to the Christian churches was in advance of the more lumbering pace of his fellow pastors and theologians, who tended to compromise and wait until they could see the issues more clearly. Karl Barth acknowledged this in a letter to Eberhard Bethge in 1967:

> It was new to me above all else that Bonhoeffer was the first, yes indeed almost the only, theologian who in the years after 1933 concentrated energetically on the question of the Jews and dealt with it equally energetically. For a long time now I have considered myself guilty of not having raised it with equal emphasis during the church struggle (for example in the two Barmen Declarations I composed in 1934).[49]

This is not to deny that Bonhoeffer's initial written reaction to the Aryan Clause being foisted on both civil and church government was cautious, weakened by two-realm thinking and, as regards theological assessments of the Jewish people, highly problematical.[50] What Bonhoeffer did achieve was to reveal his concern for his "Jewish brethren" and to provide a practical and humanitarian basis for actions by individuals against the state policy, even if the traditional Lutheran doctrine of the two kingdoms impeded him from linking the church more closely to humanitarian aims and causes. For example, in "The Church and the Jewish Question" he asserted that the church cannot "exert direct political action, for the church does not pretend to have any knowledge of the necessary course of history." [51] Responsibility for effecting any change even in the face of such blatantly unjust laws would fall to individuals and humanitarian associations. Bonhoeffer was not yet at the point of advocating that the church "jam the spokes" of the political wheel. He did see, however, the need for a responsible attitude on the part of individual Christians, who could thus freely oppose the impersonal and heartless bureaucracy behind unjust laws. [52] This essay, together with his actions on behalf of Jews in the 1930s, demonstrate his courage and willingness to speak out on sensitive and dangerous issues even as he stood in a twilight zone of decision, where nothing was clear and precise.

This decisiveness on his part was in keeping with his own sense of the importance of accepting responsibility. History, he declared, "arises through the recognition of responsibility for others." [53] This is, moreover, the challenge of Jesus in the Sermon on the Mount, a challenge that becomes operative only in the reality of history, not in the formulation of an abstract ethic. At times the decision to become involved means, as Bonhoeffer observed in his *Ethics*, to enter, following the example of Jesus, "into the fellowship of the guilt of people and to take the burden of their guilt" upon oneself. [54] Not to accept this "guilt"—which could arise from engaging in violent actions against the unjust state threatening life, freedom, and the gospel—leads only to worsening the evil and to a greater guilt. Bonhoeffer deplored the results of such Christian apathy in his confession of guilt on behalf of the church. [55] Apathy in the name of a desire to preserve one's innocence or in the name of obedience to "law" would, in Bonhoeffer's opinion, be an irresponsibility, even an inexcusable complicity in the evil being perpetrated. [56]

Although in *The Cost of Discipleship* Bonhoeffer had stressed obedience to the state except where the state interferes with faith in Christ and never counter to the "divine law" which forbids killing, now, in his *Ethics*, even this limit would give way to the freedom of a Christian to act responsibly. Given the necessary circumstances, the divine law must be violated in the name of freedom in order paradoxically to make the divine law more effective in the future.[57] In resisting evil, freedom takes precedence over obedience to a lawfully constituted state. The final referent of resistance in the name of such freedom is Jesus Christ. Jesus is likewise the model after whom all resistance to established authority can be patterned.[58] Bonhoeffer was convinced that Jesus himself possessed a personal freedom allowing him to cut through the dehumanizing structures of the organized religion and politics of his day. Christ's words and actions reflected a freedom for responsible action in the world that was capable of recognizing human obligation and genuine human values.[59]

Bonhoeffer also recognized that the ideal of imitating Jesus Christ in the important matter of freedom and responsibility was not without its own difficulty, especially in the contagious confusion of the Hitler era. He was sensitive to historical complexity in the political sphere. Hence, he wanted to avoid decisions derived from some historical *a priori* larded with metaphysical and historico-apocalyptic presuppositions. He decried the uselessness of basing judgments for action on a general theory of history rather than on the evidence of facts themselves.

Nonetheless, he realized that the "factual evidence" could be ignored even by intelligent people. The events that made Hitler possible should have alerted people to the evil growing in their midst and dictated a course of action for the church. However, the impact of the facts, though obvious to Bonhoeffer and a few others, was so blunted by the regnant attitudes of opportunism, fear, and obtuseness that a paralysis of responsibility and dullness toward the suffering of others set in. The Christian church in Germany, in Bonhoeffer's opinion, had reached the situation of *ultima ratio*, or last resort, where "the exact observance of the formal law of a state . . . suddenly finds itself in violent conflict with the ineluctable necessities of the lives of men." [60] Law and principle are of little help in such a conflict. Nor can guilt be avoided, because Christians must engage in action as forceful as the evil they are trying to destroy in order to restore the inner freedom needed to enable people to think clearly and to act responsibly. These are actions Bonhoeffer would hardly call Christian; but, given the historical situation, they are actions no responsible Christian would shirk.[61]

Faith and the affirmation of life

In this perspective freedom to act had to be linked with an increased awareness of one's autonomy. In his letters Bonhoeffer described the progression of history—with its rhythms of scientific advancement and spasms of insurrection, war, and dissolution of social order—to argue that the world had come of age and that people had reached adulthood in that world.[62] He asserted, therefore, that the world has attained a certain scientific, technological, and societal maturity liberated from primitive religious or superstitious solutions to problems confronting society. Religion, he said, is a "historically conditioned and transient form of self-expression." In this case, Christ can no longer be considered "an object of religion," if he is to be acknowledged as the Lord of history.[63] People, too, are caught up in the signs of this progress toward maturity. They have outgrown the tutelage of religion and the attitude of using God as a stop-gap solution of the seemingly insoluble or as a ready-made excuse to avoid responsibility for shaping the progress of history. Bonhoeffer declared that the emergence of human autonomy is a phenomenon with all the force of historical progress behind it. The self-defeating, rearguard action of the church against the assertion of this autonomy over against the controls of religion Bonhoeffer labeled as pointless, ignoble, and unchristian.[64]

The new power that comes to the autonomous person, however, can be as ambiguous as the events of history itself. Here it is important to differentiate between the "worship of power," which Bonhoeffer had condemned in both church and state as an effort to dominate and exploit people, and the basic human need for self-affirmation and fulfillment. He praised the achievement of the latter as a strength leading the human person in a rational, courageous, and effective manner to undertake solutions to the problems of life formerly thought to be the domain of religious ritual.[65]

At this juncture in Bonhoeffer's theological development he faced up to the challenge posed to Christianity by atheistic thinkers like Friedrich Nietzsche and Ludwig Feuerbach. Nietzsche had prophesied the death of the traditional concept of God and hence the destruction of the ethical system on which Christian society was based. His atheism, expressed in the heartrending "vision" of the madman, was the natural outcome of his conviction that, to attain maturity, a person must courageously leave behind the childhood shelter of his gods. Something new must replace God as the medium of traditional values. This, for Nietzsche, would be man, or rather, the "superior man" (Übermensch).[66] In his opinion the Christian religion was a religion of slaves, denigrating the good of human life in order to magnify God's power.[67] Man, with his power of will, should replace the supposed dictates of God by a reaffirmation of human ideals as the only true source of the good.

Bonhoeffer took up this challenge in his discussion of how a Christian must love the earth and work for the betterment of all peoples. The Christian in full freedom, strength, and responsibility affirms life, because God's manifestation in Christ has a liberating force for him. Bonhoeffer did not simply attempt to refute Nietzsche's charge that Christian morality is a slave morality; he absorbed Nietzsche's protest into his own Christian ethic. His fundamental answer to Nietzsche was that a true reconciliation with God has been effected by Jesus Christ, whose gospel taken seriously can free the Christian for unselfish action within the community.[68] A person's subsequent sense of freedom, then, produces a revolution in moral thinking along many of the lines called for by Nietzsche.

Nonetheless, Bonhoeffer felt that Nietzsche's view of reality never fully escaped the ambiguity of human solitude and estrangement, simply because his ethic did not appear to endorse sufficiently the goodness of "the other." [69] Ethical reality, he insisted, had to affirm the community of a person with others as a starting point for acceptance of and exercise of freedom in the world. This cohumanity had been embodied in Christ's life and death for others. Bonhoeffer structured all reality in terms of Christ; for him, the "superior man" of Nietzsche would be the man in Christ. He thus turned Nietzsche's premises into Christological conclusions without losing sight of Nietzsche's insight that a person must always affirm life. Taking a cue from Nietzsche, Bonhoeffer remarked that Christ "does not lead man in a religious flight from this world to other worlds beyond; rather, he gives him back to the earth as its loyal son." [70]

Bonhoeffer's critical appropriation of the thought of Nietzsche was also extended to Ludwig Feuerbach. Feuerbach had attacked the way Christianity had presented God as a vampire-like idol, sapping people of their strength in order to feed his own omnipotence. He considered this God a mere prop to human weakness and religion itself an alienating force separating people from their true place in the world. Hence he saw it as his duty to "transform friends of God into friends of man, believers into thinkers . . . candidates for the hereafter into students of this world." [71] But if, for Feuerbach, it was a question of unmasking Christianity as an ideology robbing people of their autonomy, for Bonhoeffer it was more a question of unmasking the fraudulent in religion and theology while restoring a Christ-centered perspective to the church. He argued against all false images of God and against all efforts to turn Christianity into an ideology. While Feuerbach complained that in Christianity, "to enrich God, man must become poor; that God may be all, man must be nothing," [72] Bonhoeffer depicted the paradoxical weakness of God, God powerful in his helplessness on the cross.[73] In Feuerbach's opinion, Christianity created a dilemma for people by dividing reality into the heavenly and the earthly. Bonhoeffer, especially in the latter part of his life, tried to wrest Christianity from the horns of this dilemma by attempting to do away with the "superstructure" concept, which many theologians had previously used to explain the distinctions of God and world, the divine and the human. His solution lay in recognizing Christ as the structure of all reality, so that in Christ the reality of God and the reality of the world are seen as reconciled and one is led to affirm God in what is earthly and human.

During his imprisonment Bonhoeffer realized that religious institutions had not only failed people but, by their apathy were at least partly responsible for the catastrophe of the war. Contrasting "religion" both with Christ and with the person involved in living integrally in the world, he asked whether religion had not been merely an exterior garment of Christianity, a covering that must be discarded in order for the world to attain adulthood and for Christianity to breathe again in that world. Institutionalized forms of religion seemed to leave room for Christ only at the boundaries of a person's life, on call to supply one's needs, or, like a divine opiate, to soothe the "religious" person past some new crisis. According to Bonhoeffer, religion had assumed a self-centered outlook on reality, fostering anxiety over the salvation of one's soul and purity of conscience and obscuring more important aspects of the biblical message. People who thus engaged in an anxious scrutiny of their own sins and their own spiritual exercises became "fair game" for ministers who sought to capitalize on their fears and to seal them within a confining religious shell. Instead of looking to God and the world, as the Bible counseled, the church had turned ever inward.

Bonhoeffer denounced any theory of holiness separated from life in the real world. "Does the question about saving one's soul appear in the Old Testament at all? Are not righteousness and the Kingdom of God on earth the focus of everything and is it not true that Rom. 3:24ff. is not an individualistic doctrine of salvation, but the culmination of the view that God alone is righteous? It is not with the beyond that we are concerned, but with this world as created and preserved, subjected to laws, reconciled, and restored." [74] Bonhoeffer likewise opposed all efforts to make of God the postulated answer to human weakness, a *deus ex machina* hovering over the stage of life, ready to descend to the rescue. God becomes thus only a "working hypothesis" foisted on people as substitute for their own autonomy in and responsibility to the world. [75]

To counteract this attitude Bonhoeffer called for a radical rethinking of all the basic concepts of faith and for a return to authentic Christianity. This meant rediscovering the essential relationship between human autonomy and faith in Jesus Christ. [76] Bonhoeffer depicted Jesus as one whose words and actions reflected a wholeness and integrity that were also the hallmarks of a mature outlook on life. For Jesus, this attitude could keep laws in their proper perspective without his becoming a nihilist—even though he could appear to his enemies as such—so that he and his followers could radiate a sureness and simplicity as they went about doing what they believed to be the will of the Father. This was a freedom for responsible action in the world capable of recognizing human needs and the value of others both in themselves and in the sight of God. [77] Jesus Christ, therefore, far from blocking the world's efforts to exert its autonomy, encouraged this in its amplest sense. In Bonhoeffer's view, Jesus himself presented the strongest contrast between religion and the faith that could see a blessing in the world's coming of age, even in its becoming "nonreligious." "The 'religious act,' " he wrote, "is always something partial; 'faith' is something whole, involving the whole of one's life. Jesus calls man not to a new religion, but to life." [78]

What Bonhoeffer meant by this mature life to which Jesus calls people in faith is clarified somewhat by his remarks in the letter of July 21, 1944. For the most part the letter consists in his reminiscing over a conversation he had had with Jean Lasserre when the two were students in America and were discussing what they wanted to do with their lives. Bonhoeffer said that he would like to acquire faith. At the time, he thought a holy life could secure this, but now in prison, he saw the shortcomings of such a position.

> I discovered later, and I am still discovering right up to this moment, that it is only by living completely in this world that one learns to have faith. One must completely abandon any attempt to make something of oneself, whether it be a saint, or a converted sinner, or a churchman (a so-called priestly type!), a righteous man or an unrighteous one, a sick man or a healthy one. By this-worldliness I mean living unreservedly in life's duties, problems, successes and failures, experiences and perplexities. In so doing we throw ourselves completely into the arms of God, taking seriously, not our own sufferings, but those of God in the world— watching with Christ in Gethsemane. That, I think, is faith, that is *metanoia*; and that is how one becomes a man and a Christian.[79]

An important conclusion about Bonhoeffer's attitude toward secularity immediately emerges from this letter. If believers recognize reality as "structured" by Christ, they have good reason to embrace every aspect of life that promotes human values, especially the sense of responsibility and autonomy whereby one stands in all one's strength before God. Bonhoeffer recognized the world as the place where God encounters people and acts to promote life and joy. He claimed that the Christian outlook toward the world and life can be no less than that of Christ.

That this had not been the case, he asserted, is evident from the action of "religion" to preserve a place for itself by projecting a bleak prognosis of unhappiness, sin, and despair onto the world. The ploy of many church leaders was to relativize the present, reserving to themselves the ultimate questions, which were then used in a fatuous attack on the world's maturity.[80] Theirs was obviously not the concern of the ordinary person, however, who had neither the time nor inclination to brood over his "despair" or to regard his "blessings" as an evil in disguise.[81] Nor could this be said to be the attitude of Christ, who, while demanding a reversal of the religious values then in vogue, did not proceed to accentuate life's miseries or to avoid the sinner and society's outcasts. Christ regarded a person's life, health, and happiness as blessings in themselves, because the whole of human life belonged to his Father's kingdom. This is the attitude that Bonhoeffer said must distinguish Christian faith in a "nonreligious" world. To the question, "How is the world come of age claimed by Jesus Christ?" Bonhoeffer answered, "through faith," understood in its fullest sense as a participation in the attitude of Christ and not in the restricted, other-worldly sense of religiosity and false piety.

Positively, this attitude takes the world's ideals seriously while striving to humanize every aspect of society. The Christian vocation is not to religious separatism, but to life. "To be a Christian does not mean to be religious in a particular way, to make something of oneself... on the basis of some method or other, but to be human—not a type of being human, but the person that Christ creates in us."[82] Attention to human example by sharing "in the secular problems of ordinary life, not dominating, but helping and serving," he wrote in his "Outline for a Book," gives emphasis and power of the Word of God more so than any abstract argument.[83] The relationship of faith to the whole of Christian life, then, is like the *cantus firmus* of a polyphony. Such a faith is able to take life in its stride, enjoying the blessing without always trying to transpose the good things of life into an eternal key.

Bonhoeffer considered mistrust of earthly blessings a fundamental ingratitude toward God, a sign of a lack of love. Openness to a full human life, on the other hand, was a vital part of faith. As he expressed it in a letter to his fiancée:

When I also think about the situation of the world, the complete darkness over our personal fate and my present imprisonment, then I believe that our union can only be a sign of God's grace and kindness, which calls us to faith. We would be blind if we did not see it. . . . This is where faith belongs. May God give it to us daily. And I do not mean the faith which flees the world, but the one that endures the world and which loves and remains true to the world in spite of all the sufferings which it contains for us. Our marriage shall be a yes to God's earth; it shall strengthen our courage to act and accomplish something on the earth. I fear that Christians who stand with only one leg upon earth also stand with only one leg in heaven.[84]

Bonhoeffer claimed further that this kind of faith, whereby a person recognizes God at the center of life, whether in joy or sorrow, health or suffering, is grounded in the revelation of God in Jesus Christ.[85]

Participation in the sufferings of God in the world

Bonhoeffer's insistence that a Christian is called to be a person after the manner of Jesus is one of the principal themes of the prison letters. When he wrote of the "profound this-worldliness of Christianity," however, he did not mean that Christianity should become mere humanism. In describing Christian secularity, he was careful to distinguish between "the shallow and banal this-worldliness of the enlightened, the busy, the comfortable, or the lascivious" and "the profound this-worldliness, characterized by discipline and the constant knowledge of death and resurrection." [86] In other words the term "worldliness" has a certain dialectical content. Bonhoeffer stated that worldliness is directed to both the reality of Christ and the worldly reality. His vision of reality was somewhat like a series of concentric circles whose inner core or structure is Jesus Christ moving the individual and the church to become a dynamic force within the outer circle of worldly reality.[87] Yet this world is still "under the curse." Like individual and church, it too is *simul justus et peccator* (justified and sinner).[88] Bonhoeffer was as opposed to

disjointing Christians from the human as he was to setting worldly reality in contradiction to or even side by side with the reality
of Christ. He believed, however, that where the cross of Christ
is not proclaimed in conjunction with worldliness, Christians
risk losing their perspective and making the world itself their
god. In this way, their "worldliness" would cease to be a genuine
secularity open to the human and the sacred in life.

Given this more qualified understanding of Christianity's this-
worldliness, Bonhoeffer's statements about participating in
God's sufferings at the hands of a "godless world" make more
sense.[89] "Suffering with God" is part of the Christian vocation
to discipleship. This entails a willingness to accept life's sufferings together with the joys, trusting fully in God and cooperating
with Christ in the work of reconciling people to God and to
each other by living an other-centered life of service. Christ's
reconciliation of the world to his Father was described by Bonhoeffer as both a creative and redemptive process. On this basis
Bonhoeffer wholeheartedly affirmed secularity. But even though
Jesus fully embraced the human condition in the incarnation,
and showed people what it meant to conform to the will of his
Father, and even made such conformity possible, the world has
continued to resist God. The world has, in effect, disoriented
people from their calling to be as Christ. As Bonhoeffer emphasized in his Berlin lectures on Genesis, the world, as God's
creation, remains the "fallen world," living between the "curse"
of its having abandoned God and the "promise" of a new creation
through the reconciliation effected by Christ.[90]

During Bonhoeffer's imprisonment his somewhat negative attitude toward the world, shown in both these Genesis lectures
and *The Cost of Discipleship,* shifted to the more positive side
of the dialectic. He still affirmed the "curse" of the "fallen world,"
in that this world can abandon God in order to turn in on itself.
But Bonhoeffer was then able to speak more positively of the
benefits of Christian secularity and to distinguish between a
"promising" and a "hopeless" godlessness. There can be, he said,

a certain godlessness that protests against the pompously false images of God conjured up by a fustian religiosity and against the corresponding tendency to depreciate one's "earthly" life. This type of godlessness, like faith, can clear the way for the authentic God of the Bible and eventually for the recognition of all peoples that Jesus is Lord of the world.[91]

Those who study Bonhoeffer's this-worldly Christianity should not overhastily conclude that he advocated "godlessness," even if he himself admittedly felt that, in comparison to decadent religiosity, a "promising godlessness" creates a better atmosphere for faith. The "godlessness" he lauded has its counterpart in the hopeless godlessness at the hands of which Christ's body still suffers. Bonhoeffer advocated neither godlessness nor religiosity. He was rather pleading for Christians to recapture their perspective toward the world and toward the real object of their faith. His aim remained the claiming of the world for Christ with the full realization that this can be accomplished only by God himself who reveals himself to the person of faith.

How God makes himself and his personal concern for his people most clearly known is related in Bonhoeffer's theology to two of the dominant themes of the prison letters: worldly Christianity and the theology of the cross. Both of these are relevant for understanding Bonhoeffer's spirituality; the former, because of the firmer ground faith acquires once a person is aware of his relationship with God in the strength and fullness of life; the latter, for the paradoxical reason that God makes himself known in Christ as a weak and suffering God. True discipleship demands a courage and strength to be engaged in worldly tasks without recourse to miraculous or extramundane solutions. Put bluntly, would prayer alone be sufficient to remove the evil of Hitlerism and cause an end to the war?

In one of the most paradoxical sections of the prison letters Bonhoeffer declared:

And we cannot be honest unless we recognize that we have to live in the world *etsi deus non daretur* [even if there were no

God]. And this is just what we do recognize—before God! God himself compels us to recognize it. So our coming of age leads us to a true recognition of our situation before God. God would have us know that we must live as those who manage our lives without him. The God who is with us is the God who forsakes us (Mark 15:34). The God who lets us live in the world without the working hypothesis of God is the God before whom we stand continually. Before God and with God we live without God. God lets himself be pushed out of the world onto the cross. He is weak and powerless in the world, and that is precisely the way, the only way, in which he is with us and helps us, not by virtue of his omnipotence, but by virtue of his weakness and suffering.[92]

It seems evident from this passage that Christ's cry of abandonment (Mark 15:34) became an impassioned expression for Bonhoeffer of how God wishes a person to live in faith.

The puzzling dimension of Bonhoeffer's interpretation of God's "weakness" and "powerlessness" in the world lies in the paradox of "with God" living "without God." The God without whom we live is that false *deus ex machina* or stop-gap deity, the "God of religion," all-powerful but remote, often used as a "clerical tool" to keep people unaware of their own calling as Christians to be autonomous, responsible, and decisive in the struggle for human rights. Such a God clashed with the intellectual integrity of mature Christians, scientists, men of learning and, in Bonhoeffer's immediate experience, the men of the resistance, who had come up with perfectly natural explanations of many phenomena previously attributed to interventions of the deity. In other words, the God we must live without is the childish caricature of God, which cuts people off from the real world and projects God's transcendence into an unreal beyond. Bonhoeffer proposed a return to the authentic God of the Bible, whose transcendence is to exist for others. In this more personal encounter God is related to people in their strength and exerts power only by a paradoxical weakness.

In a way, too, the theme of God's strength in weakness appealed to Bonhoeffer as he became caught up in the machinations of the political conspiracy. He "justified" the actions of the conspirators in terms of an ethics of free responsibility in imitation of Jesus Christ, who gave his life for the sins of the world.[93] The abnormal world of Nazism climaxed at the point in history when "responsible and pertinent action leaves behind it the domain of principle and convention . . . and is confronted by the extraordinary situation of ultimate necessity, a situation which no law can control." [94]

This extreme situation called for the deed of "free responsibility," which, though it might entail violence, would never erect that violence into a principle, nor seek to eradicate those laws preventing the violation of human rights. According to Bonhoeffer, persons of free responsibility must acknowledge law even as they violate it. In effect, Jesus Christ becomes their conscience.[95] "Jesus is concerned solely with love for the real person and for that reason he is able to enter into the fellowship of the guilt of people and take the burden of their guilt upon himself. . . . As one who acts responsibly for the historical existence of people Jesus becomes guilty." [96]

Bonhoeffer had decided to enter into that "fellowship of guilt" by freely accepting the personal shame of "treachery." He who had earlier advocated passive resistance and nonviolence now experienced the moral turbulence of a political, violent conspiracy. To engage in plotting actions he inwardly abhorred and without the support of either the church or the majority of the people demanded an extraordinary sense of freedom on his part. It meant enduring the shame of "betraying" his country, and the loneliness of becoming a lawbreaker. Those called to become involved in Germany's salvation by plotting its defeat in the war did so in the face of their possible death as a "dishonored witness" on behalf of humanity.[97] In this, the conspirators took comfort from Jesus, who did not cling to his own sinlessness but through concern for society's outcasts and suffering became a lawbreaker, taking on himself "the guilt of all people." [98]

As Bonhoeffer lamented in his essay, "After Ten Years," it was the lack of such freedom and a slavish obedience to their "ethics of duty" which hobbled the consciences of the German generals, leading them to set their own "sinlessness" above responsibility to the people and "to do their duty by the devil." [99] These generals, men of apparent moral principles, thus allowed the evil of an unjust war to go unchecked, even though they alone possessed the power needed to carry out a successful tyrannicide. They lacked the freedom needed to place basic human rights above scrupulous fidelity to their military oath. Because of this they waited until it was too late. They had, in Bonhoeffer's opinion, missed an opportunity to act as Christians in venturing "the deed of free responsibility" and to draw help from the example of Christ in overcoming their hesitation over the means required.

> We are not Christ, but if we want to be Christians, we must have some share in Christ's large-heartedness by acting with responsibility and in freedom when the hour of danger comes, and by showing a real sympathy that springs, not from fear, but from the liberating and redeeming love of Christ for all who suffer. Mere waiting and looking on is not Christian behavior. The Christian is called to sympathy and action . . . by the sufferings of his brethren, for whose sake Christ suffered.[100]

In sum, Bonhoeffer's decision to join the conspirators in opposition to the corrupt and criminal Nazi regime was an effort on his part to conform to the example of Jesus Christ. His willingness to suffer and die for others in the struggle for freedom from what he perceived to be an anti-Christian and inhuman tyranny became an ultimate test of Bonhoeffer's faith.

In his prison letters, as in his life, he wished to peel away the layers of religious inauthenticity which had masked true faith. The crucial question of faith for him was not "What *must* I believe?" nor even "What *can* I believe?" but "What do we really believe? I mean, believe in such a way that we stake our lives on it?" [101] The answer to that question constituted Bonhoeffer's gauge for determining whether the faith professed by Christians had indeed effected a genuine liberation, freeing them to be, like Christ, people living to be of service to others—especially the poor, suffering, and disadvantaged of this world.

4

Faith, the Liberation of the Church

Some 32 years after Bonhoeffer's execution for his activities in the German resistance, a German theologian, Paul-Gerhard Schoenborn, wrote that Bonhoeffer's church had first forgotten him in prison, then lauded him as a Christian martyr, but had ended up by making him a nonperson.[1] The reasons for this, perhaps unconscious, attempt to deaden the impact of Bonhoeffer's scathing denunciation of church inertia and outright sinfulness are many. We cannot, like some church leaders, retreat into indifference toward Bonhoeffer because of what they claim to be the difficulty of understanding the whole point of his varied, at times fragmentary, ecclesiology. Neither can we say that the church has *already* "profited" by the witness of Bonhoeffer and is now well launched into the work of reform he had envisioned. Rather, even today, he still continues to be much of an embarrassment to German church leaders.

Perceptive observers of this anomalous situation in Germany point out that in the interval since World War II, the church, challenged by Bonhoeffer to divest itself of its wealth and privileges, became, not "poor" after the example of Christ, but wealthy and status conscious. Repentance and confession of guilt were half-hearted at best. The church had once again acquired privileges and, in the scramble to recapture its respectability, had managed to convince itself that it was without blame in the Nazi Holocaust. Bonhoeffer's own "confession of guilt" on behalf of the church, composed with a timidly irresponsible church in view, would hardly find resonance among those desirous of nothing more than to maintain a complacent, lukewarm "Christian" existence. Such people do not want the "hassle" of active involvement with those who struggle against the many forms of injustice. Indeed, some church leaders praise Bonhoeffer only as a cover for their continued entrenchment in a comfortable church reestablished as spiritual power broker within Germany.

The church in the Federal Republic of Germany is, moreover, presently mired in an identity crisis, which often translates itself in poor attendance and social ineffectiveness. Such a church fears to follow the more decisive example of Bonhoeffer, lest many of the more conservative church membership be alienated and its lingering power slowly drained away. The "mission" of the church seems to be split between the enunciation of progressive theological positions, even a theology of social justice and revolution—comfortably abstract, of course—and the preservation of a certain confessional orthodoxy. In such a situation Bonhoeffer is often regarded as "a menace to Christian identity and a destroyer of the Lutheran doctrine of the two separate kingdoms of Church and State. His 'non-religious interpretation' is looked upon as one of the causes of a dangerous second Enlightenment, and his underground activity against Hitler as overstepping the legitimate boundaries of the Church's domain." [2] Bonhoeffer's heroic witness with its sociopolitical repercussions has apparently not yet been integrated into the life of his church.

Bonhoeffer remains, in fact, an enigma to the churches, which in the postwar era have regained all their prewar privileges. Instead of becoming fully the church existing, like Christ, for the sake of serving and helping people in need, these churches have preferred the comfortable middle-class faith that is eager

to preserve clerical, ecclesial perquisites, and the standing totems of their own stability. The churches are still far from that
freedom to risk everything for God and others. In a word, they
are hardly free from the self-seeking lurking behind the decep-
tive mask of "cheap grace." It seems, therefore, that Bonhoeffer's
disillusionment with his church, which reached bitter crescendo
in the prison letters, might be just as strong were he alive today.
The point now, as then, is whether the church is conscious of
its need to be an *ecclesia semper reformanda* in order to live
as Christ and to be free enough "to die" for the sake of faith in
Jesus and his gospel.

Bonhoeffer's early ecclesiology: the church as Christ's presence in the world

This sense of the church's Christic vocation, which fired Bonhoeffer's zeal for inner ecclesial reform and determined resistance to political coercion during the crisis years of the Nazi
takeover, was a natural evolution from his earlier idealistic understanding of church blended with that pragmatism which
moved him so readily to concrete action. In his earliest published work he had depicted the church as Christ's continued
presence on earth through a community of believers united in
his name. Its calling was to be a "communion of saints." But
Bonhoeffer also emphasized the empirical character of the
church. The church is Christ's presence in the world but at the
same time, as a *peccatorum communio*, a social institution composed of sinners and, therefore, constantly in need of reform.
The idealism of what a church is and should become was con-
sistently balanced by a realistic assessment of how a church had
tended historically to wander into dead ends of corruption.

Bonhoeffer's description of the church was, as in every aspect
of his theology, Christocentric and personalist. The church, he
said, was called into being by the divine "Thou" who confronts
and relates to believers as persons. On the basis of God's love

for his people in Christ, Bonhoeffer described not only the broth-erly-sisterly relations of Christians but also the ground for any possibility that the church be itself a mediator of divine reve-lation. "But since I first know God's 'I' in the revelation of his love, so too with others. Here the concept of the church finds its place." [3] Members of the community should reveal Christ to each other just as Christ reveals God to them. Bonhoeffer's un-derstanding of church depended on what he called Christ's vi-carious action on behalf of his people. Christ reconciled people not only to God his Father but to each other as well. The church is called to live out and be a witness to this reconciliation.

In developing the sociality of Christ's presence in time as the church, Bonhoeffer wanted to avoid two extremes: the *histor-icizing* extreme (which confuses the "church" with empirical-structural aspects of the community) and the *religious* extreme (which identifies the "church" with the kingdom of God).

The first of these, the *historicizing* extreme, blurs the reve-lational reality of the church into the empirical community, whose upbuilding, even through good motives of "growth in the faith," may push the more fundamental relationship with God, which is the essence of faith, to the background. In the extreme, this could move a congregation to lose sight of its identity with Christ in order to engage itself in feverish mis-sionary or conversion activity and to take comfort in the growing number of its members and buildings.

The second, the *religious* extreme, too often fails to take history seriously, either by glorifying its own historicity or by shrugging the empirical off as merely accidental to the heaven-bent mission of the church.[4] This perspective sees only the com-munion of *saints* and uses the "religious essence" of church as a pretext to avoid self-sacrificing confrontation with "God's will" as manifest in historical events. This "will of God," according to Bonhoeffer, was the judgment of Christ on the sinfulness of the church, set forth in his reminder that a church must be constantly engaged in a process of internal reform and action on behalf of others. Bonhoeffer contended that the reality of the church must include both a sense of its own historicity as well as an acknowledgment of dependence for its identity on God's self-manifestation in the person of Jesus Christ.[5]

In his ecclesiology Bonhoeffer opted for an understanding of the church from *within* its calling to be the church of Jesus Christ, "not as historically comprehensible, but as having its basis in the reality of God and his revelation." [6] He declared that the church is a revelational reality requiring faith as the only adequate criterion for judging her claims. This faith is a premise, not for empirical analysis of socioecclesial structures, but for the deeper awareness of the gospel that ensues when one is confronted by God. Bonhoeffer's point of departure for his ecclesiology is the reality of this revelation, which in turn enriches one's understanding of community relationships.[7] He derived the meaning of Christian community from the prior question of God's self-manifestation in Christ. "The Christian concept of the church," he wrote, "is reached only by way of the concept of revelation." [8]

For this "revelation" to become real for persons there was needed, according to Bonhoeffer, not merely the tangibility of history in which God acts but also the specific locus of Christ's presence in the congregation of those committed to each other in Christ's name. These believers derive their very faith from solidarity in the gospel fellowship. "Revelation," he insists, "happens within the community." [9] He added that "the being of revelation is the being of the community of persons, constituted and embraced by the person of Christ." [10] Later, in his lectures on the nature of the church, he would assert even more strongly, if uncritically, that God's revelation in the community constitutes "the whole revelation." [11]

Bonhoeffer made such an assertion from his earliest Christocentric understanding of the church. There he envisaged the church as a collective person, "Christ existing as community."

Christ was depicted as the representative of humanity, who re-
stores all people to revelational communion with God, making
possible a friendship with God, with others, and a reconciliation
with oneself—the "new relationships" of the Christian community. Here God's existence *pro nobis* (for us) becomes the
condition that makes possible that "new humanity" living in the
fellowship of faith. Christ's death and resurrection revealed
God's incarnate love at the root of all community life and over-
came the two great obstacles to human communion with God:
sin and death. Broken relationships can thus be healed in Christ,
who, as the "collective person" of the community, reconciles
people to one another and to their common Father.

The church is also the historical locus in Bonhoeffer's syn-
thesis of the "act-being" aspect of revelation. To the question
whether revelation is a past, present, or future event, Bonhoeffer
answered, all three: it is the past brought into the present and
projected into the future. Revelation is never to be interpreted
as "having happened" or to be reified into static propositions,
dogmatic or biblical. The cross and resurrection, as "eschatological events" and core of the Christian faith, are unique because they draw revelation into a "yet-to-come" model, while
guaranteeing at the same time that revelation be a "present
happening" by reason of Christ's living presence on the church.
This is so because revelation pulsates "within the church, which
is the Christ of the present, 'Christ existing as community.' " [12]

Bonhoeffer's Christo-societal concept of church, moreover,
influenced his entire theology of faith and revelation. "God reveals himself as a person in the church. The Christian community
is God's final revelation." [13] In other words, there is a certain
"finality" in the way God has bound himself to his people within
the believing community. As each member of the community
becomes a "Christ" to the other in living and proclaiming the
gospel, God's revelation in Christ occurs and is extended. Bonhoeffer depicted revelation as basically God's personal relationship to the community. Such an approach to this foundational

reality in Christian faith enables him to search out a middle path between the transcendentalism he attributes to Karl Barth[14] and the effort of "*being* theologies" to encase revelation within doctrine, psychic experience, or institution. Revelation cannot be reduced to a nonobjective, occasional impingement on existence nor to a unique past occurrence at a person's disposal, in no way connected to his individual existence. Its being " 'is' the being of the community of persons, constituted and embraced by the person of Christ, wherein the individual finds himself to be already in his new existence." [15]

Despite the loftiness of this theological sketch of the church as constituted by Christ, Bonhoeffer was also aware of the constant temptation of the church to presumption and arrogance. Instead of mediating God's revelation by living as Christ for others, the church, he contended, had tended to reduce faith to adherence to a series of doctrines or propositions and to identify revelation with either a verbally inspired Bible, as in the case of Protestant orthodoxy, or the institution itself, as in the case of Roman Catholicism.[16] Bonhoeffer refused to absolutize either the Bible or the institutional church. For him, the fact that revelation happens within the church was itself contingent upon the Spirit's activity within the community of believers. People were brought within the palpable horizon of revelation by the Word of God, which could be spoken in ways as varied as the multiple dimensions of the community's life and activity. But on one thing Bonhoeffer was insistent: God's Word could never reach his people through the church unless it were made concrete both in the proclamation and in the life of that church.

Church and state: tensions in ecclesiology

Bonhoeffer's Christocentric description of the church in his early theological writings did not altogether disappear when he began his teaching career and became involved in the church

crisis within Nazi Germany and later in the conspiracy against
Hitler. It soon became clear, however, that he had to move away
from the more abstract Christo-societal structures of his Berlin
dissertations in order to understand better the interaction between civil and ecclesial realities and to arrive at clearer, more
compelling arguments that would promote free and responsible
decisions to oppose the Nazi state and even his own church.
His early portrayal of both state and church as collective persons,
for example, could easily absorb enough mythology as to stack
any debate on resistance to their policies in favor of patience,
patriotism, and cautious inactivity.

Bonhoeffer could be patient, patriotic, and cautious, but he
was hardly inactive in resisting what he believed to be a insidious
attack on the Christian gospel. He was convinced that effective
work in the church and the future of Christianity demanded his
total commitment to help renew the church in self-sacrificing
service of others, particularly the oppressed, without regard to
or fear of the threat of suppression by civil authorities. For Bonhoeffer the main issues in the church struggle of the 1930s were
those of freedom for the proclamation of the gospel and a sense
of responsibility for decisive action against evils threatening
both human rights and gospel values. Compounding the problem of arriving at a course of action that would be ethically
sound and convincing to others was Bonhoeffer's own conservative theological and philosophical heritage, especially the
tendency in his earlier writings to accept the traditional separation of the two kingdoms, church and state, in Lutheran theology.[17]

Even as Bonhoeffer was himself somewhat stymied at first in
his theoretical working out of a Christian rationale for and tactic
of resistance in the church crisis by the Lutheran doctrine of
the two realms, his "holistic Hegelianism" helped him eventually
to overcome that traditional dichotomization of reality into separate spheres of sacred and profane which appeared to justify
noninvolvement by church in politics. He was remarkable

among German pastors and theologians in the 1930s for his ability to detect a unity between his Christian faith and the need to resist injustice in the civil realm by the best means available. Something better than peaceful coexistence between state and church, based on a mutual stand-off, was required if the church were to be true to Christ's call to responsible discipleship. The underpinning of any plan of action or critique directed against the state or schismatic church was to be, like Bonhoeffer's entire theology, thoroughly Christocentric.[18]

In his 1933 Christology lectures Bonhoeffer claimed that be- cause of Christ's presence, the church was "the center of history." [19] Such a statement, he admitted, might imply that the church might also be acknowledged the "center of the state" or that which explicitly gives both meaning and promise to the actions of the state. Bonhoeffer cautioned his students against this conclusion. Where the church had jockeyed for a central place in the state or permitted itself to be incorporated into the state, even from "lofty" motives, there usually followed some infidelity to the gospel or compromise of principle.

Bonhoeffer proceeded, therefore, to speak of the church as a *hidden* center of the state, called to be a forming influence, even if such influence were solely at a subconscious level. He added, though, that his assertion was indemonstrable empirically. In effect, Bonhoeffer was claiming that the church was called to pronounce judgment on the actions of the state and to announce that the state's ultimate purpose had already been proclaimed and fulfilled in the cross of Christ.[20] Just as Christ was the form of the church, so the church was to be a central, shaping force in both state and human history.

Such a role makes it possible for and, at times, incumbent on the church to issue the corrective and judgment that Christ pronounces against the pretensions of any state or religious institution that would abrogate human freedom. It was through the church, sensitized to a proper sense of its mission to the

world, that Bonhoeffer tried to counteract the messianic aspi-
rations of certain forms of political history. States, he noted, tend
to promise ultimate fulfillment, as if salvation could be achieved
in history apart from the inbreaking of God's kingdom into that
history. If history has any lesson, Bonhoeffer believed, it is a
word of caution against the imperialism of self-dubbed messiahs.
Such demagogues, whose pretensions were abetted by the selfishness that makes political messianism possible, had led both
church and civil society to corrupt the Christian gospel. The
promise of God in one's personal history, however, will continue
to be unfulfilled until people recognize their true Messiah at the
hidden center of human events. This Messiah has upset all the
claims of political and religious systems by his paradoxical
triumph over death. In the "secret depths" of Jesus' crucifixion
and resurrection lies the true meaning of history.[21] Bonhoeffer
saw the state both judged and upheld by the cross of Christ.
Or, as Luther put it, the state is God's rule "with his left hand." [22]
Without its "hidden center" and visible corrective in the uplifting force of Christ's saving death and continued resurrectional
presence in his church, the state would tend to overstep its
bounds, attempt to usurp the messianic role of Christ, and thus
perish in the destruction of its own order. Such, Bonhoeffer
argued, was the case with Nazism.

Given his Christic perspective on history, we can understand
why Bonhoeffer affirmed that the church can limit the state and
can even itself, as a human institution, be limited in turn. In no
way, though, could political decisions be allowed to prevent the
church from exercising its function as a critical reminder of the
limitations of all human authority. Here Bonhoeffer pitted the
guiding word of the gospel against any laissez-faire attitude toward the state.

The church proves itself to be the church of God in the world
simply by a right ordering of the message of the gospel, by a right

preaching of grace and commandment. Thus the church is concerned with giving the word of God to the world, with testifying
to the penetration of the world and its laws in the revelation of
the seriousness and the goodness of God in Jesus Christ.[23]

The state, too, can be a reminder to the church that it must
not retreat from its responsibilities to people through an "otherworldly escapism." Relating to the world is interstitched into
the church's call to be a community mediating Christ's revelational presence and urging its members to greater sensitivity in
their earthly service to others. Bonhoeffer sharply denounced
the pious fraud of religious otherworldliness, as is brought out
very clearly in his 1932 essay, "Thy Kingdom Come." In this
essay the Nietzschean influence in the form of a love of the earth
led Bonhoeffer to assert that escape into the "eternal beyond"
by being religious "at the expense of the earth" is a refuge only
for the weak and dispirited. "However, Christ does not will or
intend this weakness; instead, he makes man strong. He does
not lead man in a religious flight from this world to other worlds
beyond; rather, he gives him back to the earth as its loyal son." [24]
On the other hand, an uncritical secularity, which Bonhoeffer
defined as "the Christian renunciation of God as the Lord of the
earth," could lead to a failure to recognize God's dominion over
his creation and, consequently, is of a piece with "otherworldliness," because both lead away from God and his world.[25] One
cannot love God as Lord of the earth without thereby loving
the earth.

Obedience to God's Word exacts, therefore, an evaluation of
the earthly existence in which God operates and in which the
Christian mediates God's love to other people. "The kingdom
of God is not to be found in some other world beyond, but in
the midst of this world. . . . God wants us to honor him on earth;
he wants us to honor him in our fellow man—and nowhere
else." [26] Bonhoeffer visualized the church's role in society as an
opportunity to mediate the Word of God by being bound to the

earth and standing in solidarity with all humanity simultaneously under the "curse of Adam" and the "promise of Christ." The way was thus set for Bonhoeffer later to urge the church to affirm and try to cope with the "world-come-of-age," because this is the world, however torn apart by war, which God has loved and reconciled in Christ.

For the church to challenge both itself and a self-contained, oppressive nation state, as Bonhoeffer perceived its ministry in the Nazi years, a renewal of the church's understanding of its primary mission to the world was needed. This Bonhoeffer proposed in his address to the Youth Peace Conference of 1932. He suggested to that conference a theological basis for the ecumenical movement then budding. As he stated in his opening remarks, "theology is the church's self-understanding of its own nature on the basis of its understanding of the revelation of God in Christ, and this self-understanding of necessity always begins where there is a new trend in the church's understanding of itself." [27] Without this theological anchoring in God's revelation, the ecumenical movement would drift along without power to relate the gospel to the world. The church had to address itself to specific situations and, as a consequence, be attentive to the concreteness and contemporaneity of the gospel, avoiding the feeble generalizations of times past, which led to the incongruity of war between Christians and the fracturing of true Christian fellowship. This address had immediate application to the crucial problem of the day in Germany and the world, the issue of war and peace. In the light of the gospel, war could never be justified through appeal to the state's vocation to preserve order. It was simply too destructive of life and humanity. The state's function, according to Bonhoeffer, was solely *to preserve life and order* by protecting communities, such as marriage, family, and nation, from the chaotic whim of individuals.[28]

Years later, to express the relationship of church to state in his *Ethics*, Bonhoeffer developed the notion that all of life came under certain "divine mandates," because all of life was incorporated into the reality of Christ. "The divine mandates are dependent solely on the *one* commandment of God as it is revealed in Jesus Christ. They are introduced into the world from above as orders or 'institutions' of the reality of Christ, that is to say, of the reality of the love of God for the world and for men which is revealed in Jesus Christ." [29] No longer did Bonhoeffer call the church the "center of history"; but he did attempt to relate the church's "mandate to the world" with its inner purpose to mediate the historical presence of Christ to all humankind.

Bonhoeffer intuited a dynamic unity between church and world in which the secular and the Christian prevent each other from assuming any static independence apart from their mutual relationship in Christ. "Whoever professes to believe in the reality of Jesus Christ as the revelation of God must in the same breath profess his faith in both the reality of God and the reality of the world; for in Christ he finds God and the world reconciled." [30] Church and world are related to each other in the manner of ethical persons; each limits the other, but each must respect the freedom of the other. Responsibility and mutual service will also keynote this relationship. In such a perspective the church would stand "at the point at which the whole world ought to be standing; to this extent it serves as deputy for the world and exists for the sake of the world." [31]

The church and the racial issue in the years of crisis

In the crisis years of the 1930s, however, neither church nor world stood close enough to the Christian gospel. Bonhoeffer's personal problem became that of trying to translate his commitment to the gospel and his perception of the ecclesial-political situation into the tactics of resistance. In his 1932 lectures on the church, Bonhoeffer had criticized his church as having no fixed location "because it wants to be everywhere and is therefore nowhere. It cannot be grasped and therefore cannot be attacked. It exists only in disguise. On the other hand," he added:

> The church in forfeiting its own place can be found only in the privileged places of the world. . . . It has lost its sense of place. Now the church is hated for having occupied the privileged places . . . among the bourgeois and that spurious conservatism which clings to the old ways of doing things. . . . Its religious services meet the needs only of the petty bourgeois. The needs of the business leaders, of intellectuals, of the enemies of the churches, of revolutionaries, are ignored. It has settled down in a swirl of worldly ceremonies and has itself become radically secularized.[32]

The object of his critical ire here is, of course, the pre-Nazi church. Bonhoeffer's words, if not strangely prophetic of the coming church breakup, are at least a fairly accurate analysis of why the church would be so inept in any future crisis: it feared to take a forthright stand on any issue other than its own survival.

In the same lectures he asked where one can find that genuine place of the church in the world, designated by God's will, "where the contemporaneous Christ is present." [33] The question is not unlike his plea from prison to know "who Jesus Christ really is for us today." The point of this earlier and more theoretical inquiry into the effective presence of the church in the world assumed more concrete dimensions in the years to come, as Bonhoeffer noticed with increasing indignation that his church was not always in the place where Christ would have stood. His effort to discover Christ in the murky world of the Third Reich led him to take that long, disappointing look at his own church, especially in its timid reaction to the crises of racism, deprivation of civil liberties, and war, and to the ecumenical possibilities of the 1930s. This eventually made Bonhoeffer somewhat of a frustrated outcast.

The church's effete reaction to the "Jewish Question" was one source of that frustration. There is little doubt that Bonhoeffer's own assessment of the situation—namely, that passive acceptance of the Nazi persecution of the Jews threatened the integrity of the Christian churches in Germany—was both precocious and accurate. If his initial observations on the "Jewish Question" lacked a more daring affirmation of the church's duty to intervene when basic human rights were being contravened, he did succeed in drawing the attention of his fellow church leaders to an issue they would have preferred to ignore. After all, the Jews were not Christians; and the suggestion that anti-Semitism could in itself be prelude to the greatest apostasy from Christianity in modern times would have seemed preposterous. The church was alternately cowed and lulled into inactivity. As one prominent Protestant pastor so poignantly remarked:

> First, the Nazis went after the Jews, but I wasn't a Jew, so I didn't react. Then they went after the Catholics, but I wasn't a Catholic, so I did nothing. Then they went after the worker, but I wasn't a worker, so I didn't stand up. Then they went after the Protestant clergy, and by then it was too late for anybody to stand up.[34]

Bonhoeffer, on the other hand, was not beyond making "outrageous" statements on this issue and even urging action as the need arose. When the Nazi state had already annexed almost total power and begun its systematic policy of anti-Semitism, he claimed that "the state which endangers the Christian proclamation endangers itself." [35] That remark belonged to his essay on the "Jewish Question" in which he asked whether the "Christian proclamation" was not endangered by the Aryan Clause, which purported to isolate and ultimately to disenfranchise church members of Jewish ancestry. This essay is admittedly tinged with stereotypical assertions about the Jews and too closely aligned with Luther's doctrine of the "two realms." It likewise remains somewhat problematical in its declaration of the church's deference to the state in a period which would call for stark confrontation.

What is significant, however, is that Bonhoeffer here outlined what then was a daring course of *action* for the church when few dared to speak out, let alone act. At the least, he insisted, the church could question the legitimacy of the state's actions. Secondly, the church had an "unconditional obligation to the victims of these actions, even if they were not members of the Christian community." Finally, the church might have "to jam a spoke in the wheel" of the state through direct political action. In Bonhoeffer's opinion, this last step could occur only when the state had failed in its role either by imposing an excess of law and order or by sanctioning too little of it. Nazism had sinned in both directions; and so Bonhoeffer saw the church approaching the point where it would "be called to protect the state *qua* state from itself and to preserve it." [36]

Only later, when the situation seemed hopeless, did Bonhoeffer openly advocate overthrow of the government as a means of "protecting the state from itself." In the earlier phase of the "Jewish Question" the focus was still starkly ecclesial. What should the church do when some of its members—Christians of Jewish origins—had become, for racial reasons, victims of discrimination even within their own churches? The main issue is the arrogant, bullying interference of state in church affairs. Only secondarily does concern for human rights as such emerge as an issue—and this in bonhoeffer's reference to the need for individuals and humanitarian groups, apart from the church, to remind the state of the possible immorality of its policies and to act as the accuser when the state offends against morality. Bonhoeffer's efforts to bring the church within the orbit of the "Jewish Question" were cautious and restrained. As historian Ruth Zerner has noted, he faced the obvious tensions and dilemmas of a church leader: "Should he follow his instincts as a concerned, humane individual, and challenge the state's actions against all Jews, or should he speak with the restraint of a churchman, criticizing only policies affecting baptized Jews?" [37]

Bonhoeffer did recognize, however, the inner connection between the Nazi drive to exclude Jewish Christians from church ministry and the issue of church freedom. Surrender to the state on this point would amount to a denial of Baptism and, indeed, of the Christian gospel. Those who would exclude baptized Jews from the community would themselves in the same act be separating themselves from that communion. In short, as Bonhoeffer wrote to his friend Erwin Sutz around the same time: "The church is in very great trouble over the Jewish Question." [38] The church was also in trouble even before the "Jewish Question." Its failure sufficiently to defend the Jews or to speak up on their behalf and, at times, its complicity in Hitler's racist policies were only symptomatic of a deeper fecklessness and hesitation to be the church of Christ's gospel.

Church freedom, ecumenism, and the Nazi crisis

More than eight months before his essay on the "Jewish Question," Bonhoeffer began his lecture to the Youth Peace Conference of the World Alliance of Churches in Gland, Switzerland, with the startling words: "The church is dead." [39] Its flurry of superficial, impotent actions, resolutions, speeches he saw as only so many garlands to decorate the corpse. The church was dead, he claimed, when it forgets the New Testament proclamation of the cross of Christ. The church that sees the world reality in the superficial reality of power and progress and not in the gospel is incapable of conveying God's Word and exemplifying Christian morality to the world. Bonhoeffer wanted the church to represent the visible presence of the crucified Christ who mediates peace, not war, to a fallen world still agonizing over the ultimate question of life's meaning and death's inevitability. The responsibility of the church and the World Alliance was, "not to escape from the world, but to hear in it

the call of Christ in faith and obedience, and as they know themselves responsible to the world through this call." [40]

This is as close as Bonhoeffer came in the pre-Nazi period
toward allowing that the world itself might constitute a dimension of God's revelation. In the face of the rising mistrust between nations and the specter of another war, he demanded
that the church witness to a fellowship of peace and of peace-
makers gathered in the shadow of Christ's cross. Bonhoeffer felt
that only the church's strong sense of its brotherhood and sisterhood in Christ, as revealed in the gospel, could offset the
impending chaos.

Yet, achieving such a sense of Christian fellowship could never
be reduced to mere proclamation of church or gospel theory,
nor to the formulation of ecumenical resolutions. The gospel
meant something more specific to Bonhoeffer, who sensed that
preaching on Christian unity, apart from an equally strong sense
of the church's vocation to be a recognizable and critical presence in the world, would die the death of hypocrisy and abstraction. "The church," he reminded us, "is a bit of the world,
a lost, godless world, under the curse." At the same time, "the
church is a bit of the qualified world, qualified by God's revealing, gracious word, which . . . secures the world for God and
does not give up." [41] Furthermore, he hoped the church would
truly become the locus of Christ's vicarious action on behalf of
other people. As symbol of the continued presence of Christ in
the world, the church had a vocation to live and articulate the
gospel before the whole world. Even within the broader spec-
trum of a world continuum, Bonhoeffer tended to transpose all
the activities of the earthly ministry of Christ to his "body," the
church.

Later, then, in the period of the Finkenwalde seminary and
the composition of his two books, *The Cost of Discipleship* and
Life Together, it is not surprising to see that he continued to
eschew all ecclesial flight into "spiritual invisibility" or into acts
of faith in the abstract. Christians were to be the "salt of the

earth," a visible reality where people could enter into palpable contact with Christ. Christ would thus be made visible through his presence as Word, sacrament, and the gathering of those brought into a faith communion with his Father-God. The church's demand for "living space" within the cramping restraints of the Nazi reign of terror is, in Bonhoeffer's opinion, really its claim, not simply for the right to worship and to establish a church order, but more importantly, to live out the Christ-life of human fellowship.[42] Only from the strength of the communion does Christ extend his reign to the world.

The creative energies of the church—which Bonhoeffer wanted to see released for this extension of Christ to the world and, on the practical level, for a stronger living out of the gospel in an age under the gun of racism and bellicose nationalism—were too often dissipated by the conflict of selfish interests and fears for the loss of one's privileges as church. The problem of nationalism had become all the more disturbing to him during his year at Union Theological Seminary in New York, when for the first time he realized the absurdity of weighing one's national pride against the gospel proclamation of universal brotherhood and sisterhood in Christ.[43]

> That brother encounters brother in all openness and truthfulness and need, and claims the attention of others is the sole way in which Christ encounters us. . . . We are here and we are joined together not as the community of those who know but of those who all look for the word of their Lord . . . Christ encounters us in our brother, the German in the Englishman, the Frenchman in the German.[44]

This statement from the ecumenical conference in Gland, Switzerland, which seems so timely, delivered as it was during the political tensions of 1932, was grounded in what Bonhoeffer believed to be the only detectable bond that could reunite separated Christians: the awareness of their deeper unity in the person of Christ and their baptismal mandate to mediate Christ to one another.

From this and other impassioned affirmations of Christian unity, we can understand the fury with which Bonhoeffer attacked the German Reich church, which, in striking a compromise with nazism, appeared to have deviated from the gospel. The Reich church had thereby rendered itself incapable of proclaiming the Christian call to love of neighbor, regardless of race and nationality, in a time of confusion and widespread hunger for enlightened leadership. Bonhoeffer had himself been one of the first to join the opposition church body, the "Pastors' Emergency League," founded by Martin Niemöller. This would later become the "Confessing Church." Bonhoeffer composed a confession of faith (which Niemoller edited, though not to Bonhoeffer's full satisfaction), the "Bethel Confession" of November 1933, the first expression of opposition to the Aryan Clause which had been adopted by the Prussian General Synod on September 4, 1933, and to the nationalism creeping into the Reich church.

In May 1934, the Confessing Church, under the intellectual leadership of Karl Barth, formulated the Barmen Confession, a six-point platform that became the confession of faith for those who resisted the sanctioning by the church of Hitler's racist policies.[45] The Barmen declaration amounted to an unequivocal condemnation of those corruptions of the Christian gospel that had infected the German Reich church. Bonhoeffer contributed to the Barmen Synod only indirectly—he was pastor of two London parishes at the time—by promoting the pastoral letter of Bishop Bell, president of the Ecumenical Council, which brought to international attention the grievances of those pastors opposed to the acceptance of Nazi idolatry and official racism by the German Reich church, then under the pro-Hitler Bishop, Ludwig Müller.[46]

While Bonhoeffer was not himself present at Barmen, he did become an outspoken champion of the declaration, and in his ecumenical contacts he channeled his energies toward having the Confessing Church officially recognized as the only valid representative of the Lutheran Evangelical church in the World Alliance of Churches. He began a minor campaign against the "heresy" of the German Reich church and, because of his implacable insistence on a totally unequivocal condemnation of the heretical group and its ouster from ecumenical meetings, was considered somewhat of a young "fanatic." [47] There could be no question of accommodation for him, even to win a specious ecumenical truce between the two factions. The German Reich church had, in his opinion, falsified the gospel by accepting Nazi racist laws; they were, in effect, a heretical group undermining Christianity itself.[48] When official action on the unseating of pro-Nazi church delegates was not forthcoming, he began to turn down invitations to ecumenical gatherings until he could be given some assurance that the German Reich church would not be allowed to attend.[49]

Bonhoeffer's lonely conflict with the German Reich church in the World Alliance of Churches ended in ostensible failure. Judged in hindsight, though, his agitating role in the church struggle had a refreshing effect on the future self-understanding of the ecumenical movement. According to former Secretary General of the World Council of Churches, Visser 't Hooft, it was because of Bonhoeffer that the meeting of the World Alliance of Churches at Fanö, Denmark, in August 1934, became "a turning point in ecumenical history." [50] For the first time, Bonhoeffer's effort to goad the assembled churches finally to act as the universal church of Jesus Christ by confessing their *one faith* in the gospel had some tangible results for the status of the Confessing Church. Specifically, he had challenged the churches assembled in Fanö to address concretely the embarrassing issue of church representation. No longer should they retreat into a silence that would give respectability, albeit begrudgingly, to a racist church. The question had to be put bluntly: Was the one church of Jesus Christ in Germany to be split into a church "which in full freedom acknowledged Christ as her only Lord and hence practised fellowship with all men," and "a church combining the gospel of Christ with a pagan nationalistic religiosity in a new syncretism, which would also betray humanism?" [51] More exactly, would the ecumenical movement back the Confessing Church in its actions and resolutions against Nazism, or would the World Alliance be doomed to remain merely a movement fostering little more than peaceful church get-togethers?

Prior to Fanö, Bonhoeffer had endeavored to provide a theological basis for the ecumenical movement that might push the churches to see their more fundamental Christocentric identity as universal church and, through their ecumenical union, to become in reality the one church of Jesus Christ and a more powerful force against nationalism, racism, and war. Such an alliance of churches, he argued, needed to explore and live out that greater depth of their true identity as the form of Jesus Christ in the world. Without this Christocentric foundation and vision for a stronger, deeper union in the future, ecumenical thought would become impotent and pointless.[52] One of Bonhoeffer's complaints against the ecumenical movement, then aborning, was its inveterate tendency to "hide behind resolutions and pious so-called Christian principles, when it is called to look the truth in the face and once and for all confess its guilt and its ignorance." [53]

That "guilt" to which Bonhoeffer referred lay in its failure to proclaim the gospel in forceful enough terms and especially its failure to make it clear there are no "divinely willed special spheres of life," such as a strong nation, "which are removed from the Lordship of Jesus Christ," and, therefore, exempt from obedience to the gospel. Bonhoeffer would have preferred a silence qualified by the works of the gospel to those pious generalizations and impractical resolutions so typical of ecumenical meetings and church synods. At Fanö he asked the churches to drop their ambiguities and speak out on the gospel command, valid for the day of Nazism: to love one's neighbor, regardless of race and national origins, and to resist the pagan dilution of faith into a lukewarm mix of Bible, racial pride, and nationalism, which could only breed hatred of peoples and lead to the inevitable destruction of Christian culture.

The delegates at Fanö did, in fact, ignore strong pleas from several quarters that they remain neutral in what appeared to many Germans an internal ecclesiastical squabble. They were also cautioned against producing hastily thought-out resolutions until the murkiness of what was going on within the German church be cleared up. Accordingly, Pastor Henriod, secretary of the World Alliance in Geneva, had written a sympathetic, irenic note to Bonhoeffer in July, stating that in the present confusion the World Alliance might have to recognize that there were *de facto* two churches in Germany. Obviously he wanted to avoid being pressed to choose between the Reich church and the Confessing Church and enduring the embarrassment of having both groups openly contest the same seats at Fanö. But, as Bonhoeffer's incisive reply noted, Henriod had missed the point. If the confession of faith at Barmen meant anything, it was certainly not that the Confessing Church be designated a "Free Church" alongside the Reich church, but rather that it claimed "to be the only theologically and legally legitimate Evangelical Church in Germany." [54] Its constitution was, in effect, the same constitution now violated by the Reich church. Unambiguous approval of the Confessing Church was, then, in order.

Such a public endorsement, which finally carried in the resolution of August 30, was spearheaded by Bonhoeffer's friends, Bishop Bell of Chichester and Bishop Ammundsen of Denmark, both influential members of the preparatory committee. This resolution listed the most serious encroachments by the Nazis on church freedom and gave unequivocal support to the Confessing Church, even if it did not succeed in unseating the Reich church delegates: "The Council desires to assure its brethren in the Confessing Synod of the German Evangelical Church of its prayers and heartfelt sympathy in their witness to the principles of the gospel, and of its resolve to maintain close fellowship with them." [55]

The Ecumenical Youth Conference, in which Bonhoeffer functioned as an official delegate, likewise asserted in its second resolution that the church had to be independent in its proclamation from any "purely nationalistic aims." And, "in particular, the church may under no circumstances lend its spiritual support to a war. In the face of the increasing claims of the state, the church must abandon its passive attitude and proclaim the will of God, come what may." [56]

Aside from his behind-the-scenes maneuvering to gain recognition and support for the Confessing Church, Bonhoeffer's main contribution to the Fanö conference and perhaps to the ecumenical movement itself lay in the spirit of the Youth Conference resolution cited above. As leader of the German youth delegation he spoke inspiringly against the distortion of the gospel that would permit war between Christians. His efforts to promote world peace, rather than the resolution in support of the Confessing Church would have the more lasting effect on the self-identity of the ecumenical movement. That movement, which failed to take his cue for daring action on behalf of peace in the 1930s, in its postwar meetings contritely adopted his call for repentance.

Bonhoeffer's words on peace are preserved in the sermon, "The Church and the Peoples of the World," delivered at one of the morning services. In this sermon he reminded ecumenical Christendom that the "church of Christ lives at one and the same time in all peoples, yet beyond all boundaries, whether national, political, social, or racial." Christians may not take up arms against one another, because in so doing they would be taking up arms against Christ himself. "Peace," he said, "must be dared. It is the great venture." In the midst of the fearful silence that encourages war, and in a world "choked with weapons," and when individual churches were "suffocated by the power of hate," Bonhoeffer challenged the Ecumenical Council to "speak out so that the world, though it gnash its teeth, will have to hear, so that the people will rejoice because the church of Christ in the name of Christ has taken the weapons from the hands of their sons, forbidden war, proclaimed the peace of Christ against the raging world." [57] The effect of Bonhoeffer's words on that congregation of eminent church delegates was electrifying. Otto Dudzus later testified in his reminiscences of that sermon: "From the first moment the assembly was breathless with tension. Many may have felt that they would never forget what they had just heard . . . Bonhoeffer had charged so far ahead that the conference could not follow him. Did that surprise anybody? But on the other hand: could anybody have a good conscience about it?" [58]

Evidently some church leaders neither followed Bonhoeffer nor seemed ready to confess to a "bad conscience" in their later spiritual support of the war that ensued. Bonhoeffer, however, was vindicated on at least one issue at Fanö: the much coveted support for the Confessing Church. He called the "clear and brotherly resolution" on behalf of his brethren in the Confessing Church an action vital to the church insofar as "many leading churchmen for the first time came to see the reality of the ecumenical movement." [59] The phenomenon of German church schism put this crucial question to the ecumenical movement: could not the ecumenical movement through a council function as the one church of Jesus Christ? "With the Fanö conference," Bonhoeffer wrote, "the ecumenical movement entered on a new era. It caught sight of its commission as a church at a quite definite point, and that is its permanent significance." [60]

But the euphoria was short-lived. Bonhoeffer's enthusiastic assessment of Fanö was, as history proved, both premature and naive. Neither the ecumenical movement nor the Confessing Church lived up to the promise of decisive action against Nazism. The ecumenical movement, which Bonhoeffer regarded as the most powerful source of hope for the preservation of Christianity in Germany and the world, eventually became indecisive and unwilling to interfere further in "Germany's internal ecclesiastical affairs."

Bonhoeffer continued to needle his church into assuming ever more unyielding attitudes toward the Reich church. In the pastoral crisis of 1933, he and his pastor friend, Franz Hildebrandt, had, in fact, suggested the church revive the ancient weapon of interdict and refuse to perform any official ceremonies such as marriages and funerals. This was to focus attention on the unjust policies being insidiously introduced by the government within both church and nation. If such action meant that pastors would lose their credentials and their churches be closed or even destroyed, so be it![61] The suggestion shocked their fellow pastors. Then, as later, keeping the sacramental channels open seemed more important than Christian honor and self-sacrifice. Bonhoeffer and Hildebrandt withdrew to England in the aftermath of their frustration, there to bring the church-state conflict into the wider arena of the ecumenical movement.

Bonhoeffer returned to Germany from this species of self-imposed exile in order to assume direction of the illegal Confessing Church seminary. In that capacity he attempted to prepare the seminarians through a strict regimen of prayer and meditation and community life to accept for themselves possible loss of status, employment, or even life itself. This seminary was, as Bethge has pointed out, "highly controversial." It was, in fact, "a center for pastoral training that was strongly theologically orientated and that stressed daily worship, but at the same time a center constantly attacking any compromising and self-protective steps on the part of its own church."[62]

One such compromise, painful to Bonhoeffer and the more courageous pastors of the Confessing Church, was endorsed at what would become the Confessing Church's last synod, held in Bad Oeynhousen in April of 1936. There, backed by new restrictive laws against the Confessing Church, the Reich church committees, established ostensibly as "a guarantee that the Confessing Church's vital interests are looked after," but, in effect, to bring that church in line with the national church, offered the dissenting pastors the option of working in the officially recognized national church without having to formally accept Nazi ideology.[63] This "third way" was tempting, especially since it opened up the possibility of a ministry in parishes then closed to the Confessing Church. For Bonhoeffer, on the other hand, neutrality was only a mollified form of serving the "antichrist." In his opinion, the synod's refusal to take a corporate church stand against the bait of a "neutral" ministry within the national church was no more than a sinister cover for further weak-kneed betrayals of the gospel and of the Barmen Confession.

In such a swirl of mutual recrimination and polarization, which demanded a decision for one side or the other, Bonhoeffer's article, "On the Question of the Church Community," appeared in 1936. That it shocked and offended so many in his own church should not be surprising. It came as the climax to his claims on behalf of the Confessing Church over against the German Reich church. Bonhoeffer was eager to avoid the ambiguity so evident at the Bad Oeynhausen Synod, where the governing body, the "Council of Brethren," had caved in to the Nazi splintering of the Confessing Church into groups promoting conciliation for the sake of the "spiritual life" of the faithful and those, like Bonhoeffer and his Finkenwalde group, contesting any compromise. The point to which Bonhoeffer constantly returned in this document is the incompatibility between the Christian gospel, which grounds the church, and the national church's self-acquiescence to state domination, to the extent even of absorbing the evil policies of that state into its confession. Bonhoeffer's dossier of heresy against the Reich church had become rather thick by this time.[64] If the church was to be the community embodying the gospel, then what of a church that had fallen into heretical deviations from that gospel? At stake was not just a peaceful coexistence between churches for the sake of continuity in one's sacramental life. The German Reich church had, in effect, cut itself off from God's Word; so the

Barmen Synod had declared. Hence Bonhoeffer felt that the Confessing Church's attitude should be the recognition of the *de facto* schism in the fearless proclamation that "outside the church there is no salvation." [65] The call to salvation must, he argued, be a call to membership in the visible church, which in the steamy turbulence of Nazi Germany, could be only the Confessing Church.

In this document Bonhoeffer seems bent on forever halting the wheels of compromise by exposing the dangerous "spiritual" consequences that ministers of the German Reich church, and even members of the Confessing Church baited into compromise on the issue of Nazi church policies, were furthering. He was likewise harsh against the so-called "neutrals" who tended to hide behind mushy statements on peace and cooperation. He demanded, rather, a decision that would recognize the visible Confessing Church as *alone* embodying the gospel. In as strong a manner as possible, therefore, he declared: "Whoever knowingly cuts himself off from the Confessing Church in Germany cuts himself off from salvation." [66] Bonhoeffer saw himself struggling not simply in the political rat holes of Hitler's idolatrous, bellicose policies, which he opposed from their inception, but in the more crucial, and complex, area of faith and fidelity to the gospel itself. Outside that gospel there could be no salvation for the Christian.

The weak, playing-it-safe tactic of the Confessing Church, which attempted to throw all risky decisions involving opposition to the political authority back to the individual consciences of the pastors and laity, only served to undermine its power to witness to the gospel so evident at Barmen. Its solidarity with those members still willing to resist also faded.

The persecutions of the Confessing Church pastors in 1937 did arouse a flurry of stiffened resolution. But this, too, disappeared in the face of a new decree from Dr. Friedrich Werner, State Commissar for the Prussian church, who in 1938 threatened to remove from office those pastors refusing to take an oath of loyalty, which the church was to present as a "birthday offering" to Adolf Hitler. The Sixth Confessing Synod of the Prussian Union Church, which met at Nikolasse in June of that year, again fudged the central issue of church freedom and, on the pretext that the oath was a "state requirement," left the responsibility for taking or refusing it to individual pastors.[67]

Bonhoeffer's ensuing letter to the Berlin Council of Brethren was both poignant and bitter. "It is a heavy decision for a confessing pastor," he wrote, "to have to contradict a confessing Synod." He pleaded in this letter for the church to accept her responsibility as church and stand with the weak and defenseless, in this case the young pastors of the Confessing Church now forced to withstand political and ecclesial pressures alone. A decision by majority vote in a question of conscience was hardly a mandate and, so, the synod's decision to abandon decisiveness was, in Bonhoeffer's opinion, not irrevocable. He closed his argument with a series of disturbing questions, which could themselves have served as the basis for a postwar examination of conscience for the churches: "Will the Confessing Church be willing openly to confess its guilt and disunity? Will it have room for prayer for forgiveness and a new beginning . . .? Will Confessing Synods learn that it is important to counsel and to decide in defiance of all dangers and difficulties . . .? Will they ever learn that majority decision in matters of conscience kills the spirit?" [68]

It was that "majority decision" which prevailed, however. And so Bonhoeffer drifted into a deeper sense of isolation from many of his fellow pastors. Eberhard Bethge has described Bonhoeffer's progressive alienation from the church in these crisis years as an "inner exile." [69] Too often Bonhoeffer sensed himself virtually isolated in his rigorous running battle both in the Confessing Church and within the ecumenical movement, on the one hand, trying to persuade his fellow pastors not to take the oath to Hitler but to remain a united opposition, and, on the other, attempting to oppose any recognition of the "heretical"

Reich church in international meetings. Everywhere he saw church betrayal of the promise of Barmen's confession of faith and further erosion of the gospel spirit.

As a result he began more and more to dissociate himself from his church, which he had come to consider more interested in serving self than following the example of Christ in serving others. It was clear the church could no longer be counted on to be a dependable protector of the "weak and defenseless" of his brothers and sisters. There was no decisive church action in the religious and racial persecutions of 1937-38. There was, as he would write in his *Ethics*, no one to show compassion to the outcasts of Hitler's society, the Jews and the dissenting pastors.[70] In February of 1937, he resigned as Youth Secretary of the World Alliance of Churches. The minutes of the meeting record simply that he was "unwilling to secure a German youth delegation in which the Reich Church would be represented."[71]

The failure of his church and the events of the late 1930s influenced him, first, as a conscientious objector to military conscription, to accept a pastoral exile in New York, and, after his momentous decision to return to Germany where he might more effectively continue the struggle for freedom, to abandon, finally, the cause of Christian pacifism which he had so inspiringly championed at Fanö. These events would change his life, drawing him inexorably into the center of the political conspiracy and into the intense interior suffering that would find expression in the *Ethics* and in the *Letters and Papers from Prison*. Estranged from his church and forced into actions that would trouble his sensitive conscience and compromise his reputation, Bonhoeffer was driven into the loneliness that left him "without words, misunderstood and alone . . ." in order "to do what is necessary and right."[72]

The church's critical presence in the world

Some interpreters of Bonhoeffer's theology have seen this phase of his life, in which he was deeply involved in the running of the Finkenwalde seminary, as indicative of a desire to withdraw from the world to enjoy a comparative spiritual peace within the sheltered enclave of that seminary. They base their conclusions on Bonhoeffer's overt insistence on an unbending attitude toward church membership and his drawing of clear boundaries between the two quarreling factions of the German Lutheran church and between church and world.[73] These studies portray Bonhoeffer of this period as a theological Hamlet, torn between a divisive impulse to separate the church from the world and a humanistic urge to affirm the goodness of that same world. They cite as evidence for this some "antiworld" passages from *The Cost of Discipleship* and *Life Together*.

Marxist theologian, Hanfried Müller, for example, detects what he believes to be a break in Bonhoeffer's thought in the second part of *The Cost of Discipleship*. With Bonhoeffer's accent on obedience in the empirical church, Müller notices a "positivism of the church" and an attempt to force the gospel into a sociological and legal framework, thus contradicting his earlier stress of gospel over law and seemingly advocating a church *apart from* and *against* the world. Symptomatic of this conflict, according to Müller, is *Life Together*, Bonhoeffer's description of the community experience in the Confessing Church's illegal seminary at Finkenwalde, which Müller describes as a mere "detour" in Bonhoeffer's life and work, an ecclesial escape from the world.[74] Even Ernst Lange, in an otherwise sober study of Bonhoeffer's ecclesiology, maintains that in this book, "the relationship of the church to the world . . . becomes almost invisible." [75]

Admittedly, in *The Cost of Discipleship* Bonhoeffer advocates a definite demarcation of the church from the world and sets the church in a certain opposition to the world. Still it is hardly accurate to conclude that in this book he slips into either an otherworldly dualism or a "detour" away from involvement in the world. Bonhoeffer was writing for a church under attack by the state. He was also writing in the political ambience of a powerful government which had abrogated all criticism and had preempted to itself control over the conduct of church affairs, forcing acceptance of racist, bellicose, and nationalistic policies as the price for survival. It is not astonishing that many of his previous positive assessments of the world, and even his references to the Lutheran doctrine of the two kingdoms in his early theology—in short, anything which could in any way add to the incense church leaders were busily burning at the Nazi altar—were avoided in favor of a more eschatological perspective.[76] Nonetheless, in both books of this period there is no question of a "flight from the world." On the contrary, Bonhoeffer was struggling to establish a *critical church presence in the world*. He was a vigorous critic of the church's yielding to the seduction of the Nazi millenium. If, in the obvious context of the church-state conflict, he stressed the ultimate meaning of the church, it was for the sake of a penultimate loyalty to the earth. Even while distinguishing church and world, he insisted that "the word of God must go forth from the church into all the world, proclaiming that the earth is the Lord's and all that is therein." [77]

Life Together, wherein Bonhoeffer writes of the Christian community experiences with his seminarians at Finkenwalde and in the Bruderhaus experiment, was concerned principally with the needs of a group of theologians and students for a ministry within Nazi Germany. The seminary was beset by the dual dangers of confrontation with the rival German Reich church and suppression by the Gestapo. But, even here, Bonhoeffer was not endorsing an ecclesial apartheid for these ministers. The whole purpose of the "experiment in brotherhood" was rather to prepare the young students to function in a police state. Hanfried Müller sees this work as expressing a "catholicizing tendency" and escapism.[78] It does neither. While bearing some resemblance to the regimen of Catholic monastic orders, the communal life of prayer, worship, scriptural meditation, and confession was intended to be a spiritual vortex from which an effective ministry to the world could take place. The Christian community established by Bonhoeffer was to serve the world through the ministry of the Word but also through meekness, listening, helpfulness, mutual forbearance, and person-to-person encounter—in short, through those qualities that make genuine community possible.[79]

In his introduction—which is unfortunately missing from the English translation—Bonhoeffer emphasized that the Christian community is not intended to be the concern of a private circle but rather the work of the entire church. The thrust of his remarks was outward into the multilayered reality of human life. In the strength of his life in union with his brothers and sisters, the Christian will, according to Bonhoeffer, be able to break through the "it" world to the "Thou" of God.[80]

It would be equally erroneous to imagine, as many studies of Bonhoeffer appear to do, that the sum total of his theological production of this period is these two books. Until he was deprived of the right to function as a Lutheran minister by the Nazi regime, he remained active as a preacher, as a teacher at the seminary, and as delegate to ecumenical gatherings. In his lectures, for example, he eschewed both a docetic ecclesiology, which calls in question the church's place in the world, and a secular ecclesiology, little different from materialism.[81] From the principle that "the church is the end and the fulfillment of God's revelation in the history of his people," Bonhoeffer argued that the Spirit had to establish a visible place for himself in the world in order to reach people. He did this by exposing the community to the world and its judgment. If the church were to retreat on its own from the tension of its mission into any quasi-invisibility, it would, Bonhoeffer concludes, despise the Spirit.[82] Furthermore, in his 1936 winter semester lectures he used language reminiscent of his earlier essay, "Thy Kingdom Come," to designate the church as a part of the world created anew, adding: "And that means that the whole of life is requisitioned. It is not for a moment a matter of putting the religious before the profane, but of putting God's act before both religious and profane. . . . The church, as a part of the world and of mankind created afresh by God's Spirit, demands total obedience to the Spirit which creates anew both the religious and the profane." [83]

The foregoing citation shows how difficult it is to seize on deracinated quotations from Bonhoeffer's writings to fit some prefabricated pattern, such as would have Bonhoeffer in his Finkenwalde phase entrenched in polemics against a world from which he has somehow managed to separate himself in a monastery-like seminary. Tendentious studies, like that of Hanfried Müller, which build toward the crescendo of total world affirmation so evident in the *Ethics* and prison letters, make Bonhoeffer in this period appear regressive, almost pietistic. There can be no doubt, at the same time, that Bonhoeffer's overwhelming concern in *The Cost of Discipleship* and *Life Together* was that the church serve as a lever of spiritual and social regeneration to the world. As Bonhoeffer himself confided in a letter to Bethge, this concern could lead again to thinking in two spheres or to an attempt to avoid the "this-worldliness" of Christianity: "I thought I could acquire faith by trying to live a holy life, or something like it. I suppose I wrote *The Cost of Discipleship* as the end of that path. Today I can see the dangers of that book, though I still stand by what I wrote. I discovered later, and I am still discovering right up to this moment, that it is only by living completely in this world that one learns to have faith." [84]

This "thinking-in-two-spheres" danger seems to have been avoided in the *Ethics*, which, by reason of its Christo-universal outlook on world reality, should be considered as of a unit with the prison theology. One clarifies the other. Bonhoeffer stood by what he had written earlier, despite the danger of having his eschatological emphasis misunderstood.[85] His thought, in fact, manifests a high degree of consistency, despite the shifting of accent from the ecclesial-eschatological to the affirmation of Christianity's "this-worldliness." Bonhoeffer's *Ethics* represents his major effort to depolarize the traditional antithesis of sacred and profane. "There are not two realities," he wrote, "but only one reality, and that is the reality of God which has become manifest in Christ in the reality of the world. Sharing in Christ we stand at once in both the reality of God and the reality of the world. . . . The world has no reality of its own, independently of the revelation of God in Christ." [86] If, as Bonhoeffer insists, the reality of God enters the world in the reality of Christ, then what is Christian can be found only in this world, "the 'supernatural' only in the natural, the holy only in the profane, and the revelational only in the rational." [87]

Such an appreciative estimation of the world reality in Christ reflects Bonhoeffer's increasing involvement in the "profane," specifically in the conspiracy against Hitler. His secret work for the *Abwehr,* the center of the German resistance, brought him into contact with many courageous and high-principled persons who, motivated by love for people and not necessarily by religious considerations, had decided to risk their lives to purge Germany of Hitler and Nazism. These individuals of a variety of religious and political convictions, opened Bonhoeffer's thoughts to the more universal aspects of revelation and faith and to a goodness beyond the limits of church.

From another angle, Bonhoeffer's attack on "two-spheres" thinking can also be seen in the context of the church's exacerbating impotence against the deprivation of human rights in Germany and the conquered nations. A surprising number of his fellow pastors were leading hyphenated lives, preaching on and praying for the intangibles while retreating behind the somnolent security of Luther's doctrine of the two kingdoms to justify their inertia, to sweeten their consciences, and to survive as church. To counteract this mentality, Bonhoeffer claimed in his *Ethics* that the true interpretation of Luther's doctrine of the two kingdoms is that of a polemical unity in which Christians may and at times should oppose the secular "in the name of a better secularity." [88]

Another factor in Bonhoeffer's stress on the worldly aspects of the church's mission lay in his own ministerial situation. By 1940 he was deprived of all but furtive contacts with the Confessing Church. The consequent churchly inactivity allowed him to take a different perspective on the apologist's role he had played for the Confessing Church, whose voice in Germany had now become muted anyway. His theological outlook from about the year 1939 became ever more radically directed outward toward the universal dimensions of Christ's incarnation and toward bridging the seeming "pietistical gap" between sacred and profane.

A church confessing guilt: a church for others

Bonhoeffer's final remarks on the church are as much a plea for conversion and reform as they are a call to action on behalf of freedom. The time for eloquent sermons in praise of church and in support of peace were, he insisted, at an end. In an age of deeds and violent oppression a church reduced to "phraseology," however well shaped, could hardly be free. Freedom within a church, as within an individual, went much deeper even than the liberties made possible by democratic systems of government such as he had experienced during his brief stay in America just prior to the outbreak of war. His assessment of the American church, which he entitled, "Protestantism Without Reformation," makes curious reading, particularly in those sections where he criticizes that church's pride in its "institutionalized freedom." Despite the fact that America boasts of being the "land of the free" and churches revel in their possession of unbounded "religious freedom," he noted that such "religious freedom" had to be realized in a far deeper reality than mere "unhindered activity."

> The essential freedom of the church is not a gift of the world to the church, but the freedom of the Word of God itself to gain a

hearing. . . . Only where this Word can be preached concretely, in the midst of historical reality, in judgment, command, forgiveness of sinners and liberation from all human institutions is there freedom of the church. But where thanks for institutional freedom must be rendered by the sacrifice of freedom of preaching, the church is in chains, even if it believes itself to be free.[89]

These words could also form a powerful indictment of the church in Germany, which had put itself in the chains of a totalitarian state in order to buy a mistaken sense of freedom. In context here, though, it appears that Bonhoeffer was not all that enchanted with the "freedom" he encountered in an American church proud of its role in the land of liberty and of political refuge. Far from being ingracious or petty, his complaints about American Christianity were in keeping with his whole critical attitude toward churches in general and with his unabashed outspokenness against anything that could hinder growth toward a more genuine Christian community. To Bonhoeffer, the American church, for all its apparent freedom, was lacking both a sense of confessional identity and a proper foundation in Christology. "In American theology," he added, "Christianity is still essentially religion and ethics. But because of this, the person and work of Jesus Christ must, for theology, sink into the background and in the long run remain misunderstood." [90] He would soon leave the American scene and the haven from military conscription, as well as the possibility of a "free ministry" which it offered. Indeed, it was that very "temptation to security" which prompted him to write: "I have made a mistake in coming to America." [91]

Bethge reports that Bonhoeffer's decision to abandon the safety of a pastorate in exile and to return to Germany gave a new authenticity to his witness for Christ and church. And, even though his activity in the conspiracy would lead him to endanger his ecumenical relationships by "using" his contacts in the churches to further the anti-Hitler plot, this had the paradoxical effect of establishing Bonhoeffer as one of the great ecumenical figures in the years of the Nazi crisis. The attractive difference with Bonhoeffer was his utter integrity when so many churches and church leaders were guilty of hypocrisy and cowardly duplicity. It was an age, as Bonhoeffer had lamented in his essay, "After Ten Years," when morality in Germany had begun to collapse because of a "fundamental flaw" in the German character, the lack of a sense of free responsibility and civil courage. In their place appeared that unscrupulous obedience to civil orders and "a self-tormenting punctiliousness that never led to action. Civil courage, in fact, can grow only out of the free responsibility of free people. Only now," Bonhoeffer concluded, "are the Germans beginning to discover the meaning of free responsibility. It depends on a God who demands responsible action in a bold venture of faith, and who promises forgiveness and consolation to the person who becomes a sinner in that venture." [92]

Bonhoeffer did not hesitate to count himself among the "sinners" in the venture in freedom and responsibility that was the plot against Hitler. In the cynical casuistry of blood and conquest that was part of the Nazi ideology war and murder for the sake of nationalistic pride and racial purity were praised. The sensitive men of the conspiracy depended, however, on Bonhoeffer's spiritual guidance to support their consciences and to cope with the "guilt" they experienced in plotting the violence and "treason" needed to overthrow Hitler. For Bonhoeffer the problem became more one of accepting guilt after the manner of Christ, who himself dared to accomplish the deed of free responsibility despite the shame of his eventual execution, and of taking decisive, concrete action to put an end to all the suffering inflicted in the world at war.

In the inverted Nazi morality, unquestioning patriotism and slavish obedience to the order to kill were exalted as virtues. Yet these very "virtues" were, Bonhoeffer argued, a betrayal of one's conscience and country. True patriots were, paradoxically, those Germans who worked for the defeat of their own country. The conspirators, who were attempting to cope with the moral confusion of divided loyalties and seeming treason, were, indeed, men of extraordinary courage. "It is difficult in normal times to realize the unhappy state of divided loyalties which these men experienced, or to understand why the most conscientious person had to accept disgrace. In such a situation, however, the Christian proves himself to be a Christian. Normally, treason implies a base disposition and it is engaged in for personal advantage and with the intention of harming one's country. The opposite holds good for these men." [93]

The church had, on the other hand, opted for "patriotism" and a quietistic support of Hitler's law and order at home and nationalistic expansion by conquest abroad. Some praised the war as a crusade against atheistic bolshevism. Countless pastors seized the opportunity to demonstrate their loyalty to the state. Many enlisted. Thousands would die in the war; only twenty would die for opposing the war.[94] In short, the churches had, like the German generals, done their "duty by the devil." [95] Thereby, they too shirked political responsibility and permitted ruthless rule by nationalistic criminals to continue, supported in the respectability of church approval.

Bonhoeffer held the church responsible for this situation, because of the self-seeking and apathy whereby it justified its non-involvement in righting the obvious injustices perpetrated by Nazism. The church was either silent or a disappointing opposition to those who had accepted the challenge to deliver their nation from evil. The conspirators were forced to act in isolation from their churches. The church, Bonhoeffer declared in one of the most disturbing passages in his *Ethics*, was, by its silence, "guilty of the decline in responsible action, in bravery in the defense of a cause, and in willingness to suffer for what is known to be right." [96] Bonhoeffer's words ring with the regret at his church's having shared in the national guilt through lack of compassion and the desire not to become involved. "It has stood by while violence and wrong were being committed under cover of this name Christ."

Because of this he asked the church to confess "that it has witnessed the lawless application of brutal force, the physical and spiritual suffering of countless innocent people, oppression, hatred and murder, and that it has not raised its voice on behalf of the victims and has not found ways to hasten to their aid." His poignant confession included a powerful phrase which could itself serve as a model for acknowledgment of the church's responsibility in the Holocaust: "It is guilty of the deaths of the weakest and most defenseless brothers of Jesus Christ." [97] The concreteness and obvious repentance in this confession contrasts sharply with that self-serving rhapsodic confession of guilt by the Protestant churches in the aftermath of Germany's defeat: "We accuse ourselves of not having confessed more courageously, lived more loyally, believed more cheerfully, and loved more passionately." [98] Indeed, had they confessed with any courage at all? And how could one have believed with a "cheerful faith" in the throes of the Nazi Holocaust? What is remarkable about Bonhoeffer's confession of guilt is that it was composed, not in the gloom of the collapse of Hitler's Reich, but at the very zenith of Nazi military success—the fall of France. While the people of Germany, including many prominent church people, were milling about the streets hailing the victories of their army and the enlightened, fearless leadership of their *Führer*, Bonhoeffer was privately lamenting the church's guilt in the suffering on which the Nazi reign of terror fed.

Bonhoeffer's fundamental discontent with his church as well as his hopes for the future in a reformed, revitalized church are brought out with added vehemence in the prison letters. "The church," he urged in these letters, "must come out of its stagnation. We must move out again into the open air of intellectual discussion with the world, and risk saying controversial things, if we are to get down to the serious problems of life." [99] To Bonhoeffer the church had become a stagnant pond of general resolutions, pious programs, and "prayerful" nonactivity—all a conscience-saving cover for its feckless complicity in the war. Bonhoeffer's attitude is echoed in Ted Gill's acerbic comment on the inadequacies of the Barmen Confession of Faith of 1934: "We have little to learn from any church or any prophet who cannot recognize murder until it is murder in the cathedral." [100]

When he had given up hope for release from prison, short of a total and destructive allied victory, Bonhoeffer began a project that would take "compete stock" of the church, probe deeply into the real meaning of Christian faith, and draw conclusions for the future life of that church if it could finally be restored to credibility in the world. He devoted himself to this project during the months of August and September 1944, even taking the manuscript with him to the S.S. prison, where security was considerably tighter than in Tegel. This manuscript has either been lost or destroyed. However, the outline of his intentions and enough inspiring fragments remain to enable us to appreciate the exciting new shape he would have given the church. Certainly, his own project encompassed far more than the bland, conservative church revival of the postwar era. Thomas Day is perceptive in his portrayal of Bonhoeffer's intent as one of "clearly planning to lay the conceptual explosives within the walls of the ecclesiastical establishment, and 'in this way to perform a service for the future of the church.' " [101]

To begin, he insisted that a church hesitant to take risks for the sake of alleviating suffering in the world was a poor imitation of Christ. If Christ is "the man for others," then "the church is the church only when it exists for others." [102] What Bonhoeffer has said of the worldly involvement of the church and of the coming era of a "religionless Christianity" can be summed up in this expression. The church in the new era he saw dawning for Christianity would be a servant church defined by its Christic other-centeredness. He asked that the Christian community give radical proof of its conformation to Christ in the modern world by divesting itself of all its wealth and traditional privileges. "To make a start, it should give away all its property to those in need. The clergy must live solely on the free-will offerings of their congregations, or possibly engage in some secular calling. The church must share in the secular problems of ordinary human life, not dominating, but helping and serving. It must tell men of every calling what it means to live in Christ, to exist for others." [103] The future of the church, he held, depended on whether it had the courage to participate in the full life of Christ in the world. The life of Christ reaches people not only through the church's explicit proclamation but also by the force of example, whereby the person of Christ encounters people through the community of believers. Bonhoeffer envisioned a totally new form of church that would shed forever those religious trappings so often mistaken for authentic faith.

Unfortunately, Bonhoeffer did not have time to fill in all the details of what might constitute the "religious trappings" or of what the new form of a "religionless Christianity" could mean for the church. There are, nonetheless, enough indications in the "Outline for a Book" and in other passages of the letters for us to draw some conclusions about the radical renewal he hoped would inspirit the future of Christianity. The church would be, like Christ, a community of service to the oppressed, not an institution or structure eager to preserve status and the sources of power over others. The church would be a community heeding Jesus' call to renounce privileges and to become, like him, poor and afflicted. In this way the advent of suffering in the form of persecution or even death could be welcomed as a sign of God's continued presence in the church.[104] To be a true church, this community had to "share in the sufferings of God at the hands of a godless world." [105] Christians had to "stand by God in his hour of grieving." [106] But Bonhoeffer's church, like the disciples in the garden, had slipped into a deep, escapist sleep, to awaken only in a pell-mell flight for survival. Bonhoeffer denounced the retreat of the churches behind the outer perimeter of religion as hardly a true participation in the life of the suffering

Christ. "It is not the religious act that makes the Christian," he declared, "but participation in the sufferings of God in the secular life. That is *metanoia*: not in the first place thinking about one's own needs, problems, sins, and fears, but allowing oneself to be caught up in the way of Jesus Christ." [107]

This way would be free from ecclesiastical dissimulation and open to a rediscovery of honesty in life through the force of human example, which, unlike "abstract argument," "gives its word emphasis and power." [108] Responsible Christians are not those who try to escape into the world of a "safe" transcendent or who await a religion-sent *deus ex machina* to solve the problem of human suffering. They are, rather, those who have realized the "Station on the Road to Freedom" that dares "to do what is right," understanding that "freedom comes only through deeds, not through thoughts taking wing." [109] The church of the future was to epitomize before the world the freedom in responsibility that characterized Jesus' own life and that would shape history according to the Christian gospel. Bonhoeffer's call to church honesty in the war years is not unlike that penned by George Bernard Shaw at the outbreak of the First World War:

In no previous war have we struck that top note of keen irony, the closing of the Stock Exchange and not of the Church. The pagans were more logical: they closed the Temple of Peace when they drew the sword. We turn our Temples of Peace promptly into temples of war, and exhibit our parsons as the most pugnacious characters in the community. I venture to affirm that the sense of scandal given by this is far deeper and more general than the Church thinks, especially among the working classes, who are apt either to take religion seriously or else to repudiate it and criticize it closely. When a bishop at the first shot abandons the worship of Christ and rallies his flock round the altar of Mars, he may be acting patriotically, necessarily, manfully, rightly; but that does not justify him in pretending that there has been no change, and that Christ is, in effect, Mars. The straightforward course, and the one that would serve the Church best in the long run, would be to close our professedly Christian Churches the moment war is declared by us, and reopen them only on the signing of the treaty of peace.[110]

This can mean no more and certainly no less than that the Christian church should accept its own foundational identity with the gospel of peace and love. When, as his life drew to its final days, Bonhoeffer did his own "stocktaking of Christianity," he saw the church standing up for the church's cause but not for that of humanity—and this because it had "little personal faith in Christ." [111] It was a "church on the defensive," lacking heart to take Christlike risks for others. Hence Bonhoeffer concluded that "the church is the church only when it exists for others." [112]

His practical suggestions for renewing the church, which we have cited above, have often been quoted but politely ignored by the churches themselves, still anxious about their status and committed to political quietism. Bonhoeffer's vision of the church radically renewed as a prophetic witness to the world if taken seriously, constitutes a radical program for church and clergy. So, too, the challenge of his life and death on behalf of human freedom. It may be too early to conclude that Bonhoeffer's dream of a renewed, Christ-oriented church is too risky and unreal for the Christian churches and comfortable, bourgeois Christians. Bonhoeffer had taken the Sermon on the Mount seriously. He also took the claims of the church to be an *alter Christus* to the world literally. In this lay both his disappointment and his hope. He longed for the rebirth of Christianity while imprisoned in a world where the gospel's razor edge of love for all people and a faith true to life had been dulled. Yet he realized, as we read in his baptismal sermon from prison, that the church, "which has been fighting in these years only for its self-preservation, as though that were an end in itself," had become "incapable of taking the word of reconciliation and redemption to mankind and the world." This was a church in need of conversion and purification.

He was convinced that being a Christian in that day—and possibly this—would be "limited to two things: prayer and doing justice among people. All Christian thinking, speaking, and organizing must be born anew out of this prayer and action." In these, too, lay the possibility of the church's eventual conversion. Until that time, he concluded, "the Christian cause will be a silent and hidden affair, but there will be those who pray and do justice and wait for God's own time." [113] In the next chapter we will look more closely at these concepts in the overall context of Bonhoeffer's spirituality.

5

Freedom and Discipline: Rhythms of a Christocentric Spirituality

Bonhoeffer's life of faith, like his whole understanding of Christian spirituality, was thoroughly centered in the person of Jesus Christ. For him, Christ was the very embodiment of what it meant to live as a believing, loving Christian within a community. His question from prison, "Who is Jesus Christ really for us today?," reveals his lifelong concern to discover the presence of Christ, not simply in the people who would enter his life or who would command his compassion, but also in the historical events that had led him to prison, a willing conspirator against an unjust regime. Somehow amid the loneliness and suffering he experienced in the work of the resistance, there stood the solitary figure of Jesus Christ, the "man for others," who filled Bonhoeffer's world with meaning and liberated him to take part in the struggle against the forces of human oppression in both state and church.

Liberation in Christ

Bonhoeffer believed so intensely in Jesus Christ, whom he described as the center of his person and, indeed, of all history, that as his life became more involved in the ecclesiastical and political strife, he felt progressively freer to question many of his former beliefs because they seemed so un-Christlike in their focus. For one, he spurned what he considered the misleading "religious trappings" of Christianity. The God of extramundane solutions to life's problems, the so-called "stop-gap God" or *deus ex machina* was unreal to him. God had to be more than a last resort solved of seemingly insoluble problems.

His dissatisfaction extended also to the aloof, unattainable, self-satisfied God, smug in his heaven. A God beyond the human pathos of his creatures, the final answer to the unanswered (often unasked) human questions, may be the "God of religion" but hardly the God who had become flesh in Jesus.

Nor could Bonhoeffer bring himself to believe any longer in a God who inspired the clergy to "religious blackmail" of his people at the remote corners of their conscience where sin and guilt still lurked. God as the merciless hunter and judge of wretched sinners did not exist for him.

Neither did a God with all the answers to human suffering. God would not rescue his people from the evils of war, atrocities, and death. He came among them to live, suffer, and die, fully sharing in their human condition.[1]

For this reason Bonhoeffer constantly urged his church to rediscover for itself the freedom of Christ, even as it was being constricted in the crushing vise of nazism, and to reaffirm its Christic vocation to solidarity with the suffering and oppressed of the world. Disciples of Christ are those called to accept even their own death for Christ, not as the end of all their hopes, but as the "last station" to true liberation.[2]

Bonhoeffer saw his life's purpose as one of helping his church and fellow conspirators realize the freedom that characterized the mission and ministry of Jesus Christ. Jesus invited people to be free again in a new kind of relationship with his Father, not cramped by minute attention to law, but moved by their love for each other and "for the least of his brethren," those affected by Nazi persecution. Only those liberated by deep, interior con-

viction of their acceptance by God, though they be sinners confronted with choices repulsive to their conscience, would be
able to venture the mature, courageous deeds of responsibility
for others that could deliver a nation and a world from evil.
Jesus could set his word even above that of the religious leaders
of his day, forgive sins, and exercise compassion at the sight of
human need, though this meant "violating" the Sabbath, and
maintaining a fellowship with known sinners. He conveyed hope
and inspired faith despite the scandal his life-style and healing
activity aroused in the self-righteous. He was a truly free person
and, therefore, able to be a loving brother toward all, especially
the victims of disease and social ostracism. He was notably free
from an overreverence for the status quo and personal or institutional survival. His attitude, which seemed to declare the
relativity of law and orderly societies, brought him into ineluctable conflict with the religious and political authorities and
eventually to his arrest and execution. He threatened the whole
system of dependence on legal initiative and authoritarian sanction of all actions, a system that paraded under the enticing guise
of security and order. Small wonder that Bonhoeffer saw in Jesus'
life and death the courage that might jolt the German generals
out of their "duty-oriented," slavish obedience to their military
oath and the evil dictator.

And when the conspirators' efforts failed? Here, too, Bonhoeffer knew that Jesus' death only pointed up the fact that the
Father did not provide the legions of angels to the rescue. Jesus
himself was not to be delivered from his sufferings. God does
not save Christians and Jews from evil reprisals, even when it
is a question of the death of his own children on the traitors'
scaffold, where criminal and martyr are hardly distinguishable.
He will join his people in their suffering. The cost of the mature
spirituality that Bonhoeffer discerned in the Sermon on the
Mount was the willingness to follow Jesus even to this kind of
death. If the cross of Jesus is a condemnation of injustice, hatred,
pride, and deceit, the resurrection was the vindication of Jesus'

own ministry, which led to the realization that love is stronger than hate and life in Christ will triumph over every death. Jesus died at the rough edge of despair, yearning for deliverance but crying out a final prayer of trust, commending his spirit to his Father. His trust was vindicated in resurrection, when the in-rushing Spirit filled him with the glory that was always his. Jesus' example and words were not lost on Bonhoeffer who could say, as he confided in a farewell message to Bishop Bell, that his impending execution was indeed the end but for him it was also the "beginning of life." [3]

Bonhoeffer's spirituality pivoted, accordingly, on courageous deeds in imitation of Christ as well as on the trustful prayer of a Christian. When people attain a truly mature spirituality, they show this especially in the manner of their love of neighbor and by their courage in working for peace and justice in society. The only faith that liberates is that inspirited by love and shaped in service. Anxiety over security, survival, and even self-respect was hardly a mark of the freedom of Christ, who could move openly with sinners and compassionately touch the leper, the insane, the epileptic, and all those beyond the margins of "re-spectable society." Moreover, despite the cajoling counter-per-suasions by family and apostles and the threat of imprisonment and death, Jesus condemned the hypocrisy of Jerusalem's reli-gious leadership. The Christic parallels with Bonhoeffer's ethical decisions to break with his church, so comfortably caught in the web of national heartlessness and to enter the conspirators' "fellowship of guilt" are apparent enough in his final writings.[4] The war years were, as he put it in his baptismal sermon, the time for "doing justice" and for prayer.[5]

The "discipline of the secret": liberating religion from itself

Bonhoeffer's letters reveal something of the intense interior life of prayer and worship that sustained him in the distress of imprisonment. His "participation in the sufferings of God in the world," as also vicarious action on behalf of the "most defenseless of Christ's brethren," [6] necessarily included for him those moments of communing with God within the Christian community, which bring to explicit awareness the whole meaning of existence in terms of an ultimate. He felt that from this prayer to God and service to people would come a new form of church and a rebirth of God's Word. "It is not for us to prophesy the day (though the day will come)," he wrote, "when men will once more be called so to utter the Word of God that the world will be changed and renewed by it. It will be a new language, perhaps quite nonreligious, but liberating and redeeming—as was Jesus' language; it will shock people and yet overcome them by its power; it will be the language of a new righteousness and truth, proclaiming God's peace with men and the coming of his kingdom." [7]

The clue to what Bonhoeffer meant by the "new language" that both liberates and shocks might lie in the words immediately following that passage in the letters and in the context of his vision of a "nonreligious" Christianity.[8] Bonhoeffer's prediction that in the future era, "the Christian cause will be a *silent* and *hidden* affair," is significant because it is related to the whole problem of how prayer and worship are to be integrated into Christian life in any future renewal of church and world.[9]

By way of suggesting a practical tactic in such renewal, Bonhoeffer advocated explicitly a practice of the early church, the "discipline of the secret" (*Arkandisziplin*).[10] His first mention of this in the letters indicates that he regarded the "discipline of the secret" as the counterpart of a "nonreligious interpretation" of the Christian message. In fact, immediately after raising the issue of a possible "religionless Christianity," he concluded: "In that case Christ is no longer an object of religion, but something quite different, really the Lord of the world. But what does that mean? What is the place of worship and prayer in a religionless situation? Does the 'secret discipline', or alternatively the difference . . . between penultimate and ultimate take on a new importance here?" [11] In his next letter, after criticizing Barth for lumping all doctrines of the Christian religion in a "take-it-or-leave-it" package, he claimed that this would be unbiblical. "There are degrees of knowledge and degrees of significance; that means that a *discipline of the secret* must be restored whereby the *mysteries* of the Christian faith are protected against profanation." [12]

The discipline of the secret in the first instance, is alternated with the distinction Bonhoeffer made in his *Ethics* between penultimate and ultimate. These are terms employed by Bonhoeffer in place of the more familiar "natural-supernatural" distinction of traditional church dogmatics. Because the Christian belongs wholly to this world, after the manner of Christ incarnate, the penultimate includes a wholehearted embracing of all human values. But this penultimate living is, in turn, conditioned by the ultimate.[13] Bonhoeffer was careful that the concept of the ultimate should not be made to intrude imperiously on the penultimate in situations in which the Christian can only wait and hope for insight into the full meaning of an event shrouded in historical ambivalence. It is on such occasions that Bonhoeffer counseled and practiced a respectful silence that is akin to the "discipline of the secret" mentioned in the letters. Hence he asks us in his *Ethics*:

> Why it is that precisely in thoroughly grave situations, or instances when I am with someone who has suffered a bereavement, I often decide to adopt a "penultimate" attitude, particularly when I am dealing with Christians, remaining silent as a sign that I share in the bereaved man's helplessness in the face of such a grievous event, and not speaking the biblical words of comfort which are, in fact, known to me and available to me.[14]

Bonhoeffer was equally concerned, on the other hand, that this sense of the ultimate should never be lost in a swirl of secular activity for its own sake. And so he returned to the tradition of the early church, which had attempted to preserve both a sense of the "sacred" and respect for the "Christian mysteries" against secular or pagan profanation. In this matter, though, he is just as eager to preserve these "mysteries" against *religious* profanation." The words of Christians and their self-righteous pretensions have lost any claim to credibility in an era of gospel spoliation through acts of injustice perpetrated by Christians and abetted by the churches. Bonhoeffer insisted that the Christian life of dedicated service to others in the world be always accompanied by an attitude of faith nourished in prayer.

It is a misinterpretation of Bonhoeffer to imagine that "nonreligious" Christianity would preclude community worship or that social service could ever replace prayer and the sacraments.[15] The "religionless world" was not identical with Christianity in his theology; nor was "religionless Christianity" identical with a "churchless Christianity." Bonhoeffer was convinced that a community of faith practicing the *Arkandisziplin* was needed to prevent Christians from losing their Christlike identity in the midst of their solidarity with the "world-come-of-age."[16] This discipline was essential, but it was to remain a *secret* affair, not to be brandished triumphantly before or forced upon an unwilling world. This discipline was to help a church become liberated from itself. "Christ's remaining with us and our remaining by Christ delivers us from all stagnation in religious forms. Our bond with Christ is arcane, in that even though we may be chosen and favored, we don't make this a matter of privilege or of a religiously separate existence. It is part of this *arcanum* that I hold to preaching, baptism and the eucharist, that I worship, confess and give praise within the community."[17]

The same is true—and this is the point of Bonhoeffer's wish for a "discipline of the secret" to preserve the "mysteries" of the Christian faith from profanation—for the main dogmas of the Christian faith. These are to be maintained, but where it is impossible to relate these concepts to the world, a tactful silence is better than mere repetition of words whose cultural conditioning may have rendered them meaningless. The mysteries of the Christian faith cannot be forced on people. They await the advent of the Spirit. The relationship between the world and God's Word, which will enlighten those mysteries to the world, is an event dependent on the Spirit's creative activity and the church's prayerful listening to the signs of the present in the hope of the future and not on any mere slavish repetition of traditional Christian doctrine.[18] As one contemporary ethicist has commented,

> Arcane discipline means in part that the Church and worship in a world-come-of-age is not for everyone. It is only for the small groups of clearly committed Christians who comprise an intense community on the basis of their common, intense loyalty to Christ; and their expression of the meaning of that loyalty and community is communicated to and with one another in worship. . . . Worship as arcane discipline is not for the streets, for the posters, for the media, for the masses. It is certainly not Hollywood Bowl and Drive-in Easter sunrise services, nor Sunday East Room exercises in American civil religion, nor Astrodome rallies or religiosity. . . . It is not bumper-sticker and slick-paper Christianity. The Church, if Bonhoeffer has his way, will be rigorous in its membership stipulations and devout in its practice of disciplines. It will also give up its property for the sake of the needy." [19]

The "discipline of the secret" seems to be interrelated with Bonhoeffer's concepts of mature worldliness and the issue of a "nonreligious interpretation" of Christian concepts. These would serve as mutual correctives. Many of the revelatory insights of a church aware of God's living word in the patterns of her growth into Christ are already open for a "nonreligious interpretation." Where this interpretation is either impossible or unacceptable, the church continues to preserve the mysteries of the Christian faith, not with a pathetic defensive fervor, but with prayer, worship, and example. The church's understanding of God depends as much, if not more, on this prayer and example than on any effort at an explicit "nonreligious interpretation" of its faith. Further, the "discipline of the secret" is intended to insure the Christic perspective of all vicarious action of the church on behalf of others. For Bonhoeffer, Christ is as much the center of the "discipline of the secret" as he is the structure of all reality and the responsible life. Christians pray and worship in a fellowship of believers and thus strengthen those attitudes that enable them to serve others in creating a better human life. If the same Christ-oriented outlook is not shared by everyone, the Christian nonetheless continues to trust that the Holy Spirit will eventually give revelatory sound to his silence and example and bring the church once more to speak effectively to the world.

"Nonreligious" Christianity: freedom for the Word of God

When all the aspects of Bonhoeffer's description of "nonreligious" Christianity and his call for a "nonreligious interpretation" of biblical concepts are pieced together to include the prayer and worship of the "discipline of the secret," a basic ambiguity in his use of the word "religion" becomes apparent. One wonders whether he was speaking of the absence of *religion* or the absence of *religiosity*. His concept of *religion*, so strongly influenced by Nietzsche, Feuerbach, and Barth,[20] signifies many things that are inimical to genuine faith: excessive introspection, thinking in terms of two isolated spheres of sacred and profane, refusing to recognize the Christological structure of the world reality, efforts to manipulate God and to justify oneself, and so on. The list could be broadened to include all the deviations and unfortunate cultural accretions that have set deeply into religious institutions with the especially unfortunate result that people have often confused the structures of religion with both revelation and faith.

In general, Bonhoeffer criticized "religion" for its having inflicted on people a psychic posture of weakness and immature dependence. In his view this manifests itself, first, in the way "religion" seems to push Christ to the margins of real life, where fear of sin and death hold a tenacious grip over peoples' consciences and a military oath can contravene resistance to evil. Instead, Bonhoeffer advocated that we affirm Christ's presence as the very center of our whole life and strength.[21]

Secondly, he thought that the individualistic and self-centered attitudes of religion only turn people away from a sense of their own solidarity with and ethical responsibility to the broader human community. Such focus on self spins a person off life's true course into an escapist and narcissistic otherworldliness.

Furthermore, he construed "religion" as an attempt to thwart a person's awareness of his growing independence and autonomy by counter arguments which are intellectually dishonest and humanly debasing. "Religion," he argued, had unwittingly packed both Christ and human awareness into a deep-freeze where timeless dogma and unchanging law were more important than growth into a more mature adulthood and the responsible exercise of freedom.

Finally, "religion" seemed to foster such a preoccupation with one's own personal salvation that, to Bonhoeffer, it overshadowed true transcendence after the imitation of Christ by its very "denial of the sociality of Christ and humanity." [22]

If Bonhoeffer's reasoning is correct, "religion" had offered a God of power and the enticement of an escapist salvation myth as a compensation to humans now all too aware of their own helplessness. Lost in the unreal world of "religion" were the real sources of human strength: Christ's paradoxical power in weakness and the true freedom to be experienced when one has learned to be like Christ, a person whose life was spent in serving others in those deeds of mutual love that make the Christian community possible and Christianity credible. Yet, in Christ, not in "religion," Bonhoeffer had found the solution to the problem that had dogged him from the very beginning of his theological reflections, namely, how he could himself be liberated from the dominating power of his own ambitious, self-seeking ego in order to commit himself totally to Christ and, through accepting Christ's paradoxical strength in suffering, to engage in danger-defying actions for others.

The change in his outlook, catalyzed as much by the circumstances of his imprisonment as by prayerful reflections on his short life, had widespread implications for the way he would have the church confront the established political order. Bonhoeffer's negative judgment on "religion" and church was conditioned, moreover, by the example of the courageous people with whom he worked in the resistance, who apparently lacked the support of organized religion. Their "religionlessness" he appreciated all the more against the backdrop of the scandalous image of so many of his fellow church members, who had compromised their faith in an anxious scramble for self-preservation.

Bonhoeffer's concept of religion is obviously broad, too broad; but it is also narrow. Religion for him connoted what is pejorative in the development of those bureaucratic structures which facilitate devotional practices and attempt to regulate conformity to the dictates of ecclesiastical government. For him, as for Barth, the word "religion" served as contrast to the characteristics of genuine faith, just as the genuine experience of God must be distinguished from the attempt to fix and control that experience through propositions or statements in Bible, dogma, or law.

Bonhoeffer's failure to use the word more critically, however, has led to considerable confusion among his interpreters. When he wrote about the possible advent of a "religionless Christianity" and the opportunities this creates for authentic Christian living, he was not thereby tossing out the "religious" concepts of transcendence or the sacred. His plea for a return to the "discipline of the secret" is a strong argument for concluding that Bonhoeffer maintained the sense of both the ultimate and the sacred which we have traditionally associated with the word *religion*.

And this is the point. The Bonhoefferian term "religion" is too narrow to prevent ambivalence. In the name of a more genuine faith, Bonhoeffer set up an antinomy of *faith* and *religion*. But in doing so, he has appeared to some of his critics to jettison many aspects of religion that have made it a human phenomenon, a quality of the human person as such. At times his attitude toward religion seemed hostile. It is not always clear in the prison letters that he was denouncing those forms of religiosity and narrow-minded ecclesialism that would masquerade as true faith.

One interpreter of Bonhoeffer's ethics has attempted to unscramble the confusion in his very perceptive remark that "there will never be for man a religionless time. But there can be times in which the pseudo-religion of one human ideology or another prevails, times in which living faith is stifled by ecclesiastics dedicated to the preservation of cadavers, or by naturalists who 'in their pursuit of the temporal' surrender the eternal. Against such eventualities only the wisdom of Christ can be our guide. Only Christ, who has so intensely united the divine and the human, can finally lead us beyond our own folly and vanity, whether it be that of otherworldly piety, or this-worldly atheism, to true religion and genuine faith." [23] Certainly this assertion is not far from Bonhoeffer's own desire that the church be renewed in faith and integrity. If we contend that religion can and does fulfill a basic human need to exteriorize and communicate our faith, we must also keep in mind that, with Bonhoeffer, it is Christ's presence at the center of life and faith, not religiosity nor an efficient, bureaucratic church, which enables a Christian community to function in prayer, worship, and Christ-centered action on behalf of others.

A page from his diary of 1939, indicates Bonhoeffer considered the churches, even in America, far from being Christ-centered in their so-called freedom, stalled in that self-serving religiosity he had condemned as un-Christian and escapist. He laments that worship in a prominent New York church seemed,

... a respectable, self-indulgent, self-satisfied religious celebration. This sort of idolatrous religion stirs up the flesh which is accustomed to being kept in check by the Word of God. Such sermons make for libertinism, egotism, indifference. Do people not know that one can get on as well, even better, without 'religion'—if only there were not God himself and his Word? Perhaps the Anglo-Saxons are really more religious than we are, but they are certainly not more Christian, at least, if they still permit sermons like that. I have no doubt at all that one day the storm will blow with full force on this religious hand-out, if God himself is still anywhere on the scene.[24]

Bonhoeffer's impressions of that church service read, indeed, like a critique of American "civil religion" in general. The church he had attended that Sunday must have appeared as comfortably bourgeois and as self-righteous as it was contented in its own cautious blandness.

This was not Bonhoeffer's first encounter with the apathy that served as a shield for the churches against any prophetic disturbance of their peace. What he missed in the service was the biblical focus on Christ's Word and judgment against the "rubbish" which posed as genuine religion. He had had enough of the pretentious claim that because America was truly the "land of the free," the people there enjoyed an unparalleled independence and freedom in both preaching and churchly religious life. True enough, if this meant the "possibility" of unhindered activity by the churches. But certainly not enough of the truth, if freedom meant that God's Word should resonate in all churches with the strongest cadences of judgment, command, forgiveness, and liberation. This was hardly a church transformed totally into the image of Christ, who was free to confront the smug values of both civil and religious society and to die for his audacity. No church true to itself could become a mere echo of those values of secular society that never reach beyond institutional limits or the freedom simply to exist as church. When a church rendered its timid homage to state order and powerful persons in positions of status and wealth by a watering down of the gospel, this church was "in chains," no matter how loudly it proclaimed its freedom.[25]

Not long after the sermon which rankled Bonhoeffer so much that Sunday in June 1939, he noted in his diary:

> The Americans speak so much about freedom in their sermons. Freedom as a possession is a doubtful thing for a church; freedom must be won under the compulsion of necessity. Freedom for the church comes from the necessity of the Word of God. Otherwise it becomes arbitrariness and ends in a great many new ties. Whether the church in America is really "free," I doubt.[26]

Freedom in the prayer of silence and the fellowship of prayer

Bonhoeffer's decision to return to Germany before the outbreak of war, there to join the resistance, was an outgrowth of the very freedom he saw lacking in his short second encounter with the American church. It was a decision born of the "time to think and to pray" about his situation.[27] It was, as Bethge has remarked, "the freedom of a man who has obeyed the call of his destiny . . . the freedom of a man who can forfeit his respectable, theological and ecclesiastical reputation, even his reputation as a patriot. . . ." [28] He took the step, as he would write in a poem from prison, trusting in the Word of God whose command he faithfully followed.[29]

This Word, which became so disturbingly real amid all the apparent contradictions of his "Christian" involvement in the political conspiracy, was not that heard in the pulpit so much as a Word encountered in the silence of meditation and in the fellowship of concern for others. In the stillness of this reflection Bonhoeffer found "the focal point of everything which brings inward and outward order into his life," namely, prayerful meditation on the Word of Christ, which kept him "in the saving fellowship of the community." [30] Bonhoeffer knew from his own life and personal conviction that Christian ministers had to enter into a "daily, personal fellowship with the crucified Jesus Christ" lest their proclamation of the gospel drift into pious, shallow platitudes, and inoffensive generalities.[31] Ultimately, Bonhoeffer saw himself being led into an ever-deepening relationship with Christ in whose cross he experienced the full depths of his calling to be a minister of Christ's Word to the world.

From his daily communion with that Word, source of both inner peace and restlessness in the combat zone of German Christianity, came the strength of his own sense of Christ's brotherhood and sisterhood and liberation from the religious verbiage which had reduced prayer and preaching in the churches to self-serving piffle. True fellowship, he insisted, becomes "a question of whether we are daily guided by the image of the crucified Christ himself and allow ourselves to be called to conversion. Where the word descends, so to speak, directly from the cross of Jesus Christ himself, where Christ is so present to us that frankly he himself speaks our word, there alone can we banish the dreadful danger of pietistical chatter. But who among us lives in such a fellowship?" [32]

Such prayer in solitude and fellowship in God's Word were, in fact, the very soul of Bonhoeffer's spirituality. This was the sustenance which carried him through the years of crisis and imprisonment. In his daily meditative silence in God's presence he discovered paradoxically the great strength in fellowship of a Christian community. "Only as we are within the fellowship can we be alone, and only he that is alone can live in fellowship." [33] True, the faith community is equally nurtured by "the physical presence of other Christians," who are "a source of incomparable joy and strength." But these, too, were never absent from his prayers and reflections. If Bonhoeffer's most difficult and courageous decisions needed the support of God's concrete command in Christ, they were, likewise, decisions made in a sense of communion with both victims of Nazism and antigovernment conspirators and in the desire to share in their task and trials.[34] "We are," as he confided to Bethge, "in a fellowship that sustains us. In Jesus God has said Yes and Amen to it all, and that Yes and Amen is the firm ground on which we stand." [35]

His own sense of solidarity with his family and friends welled up naturally into a plea for their intercessory prayers. They were a fellowship united in a dangerous ministry, to be sure, but they were likewise Christians linked by their common embrace in faith at the foot of Christ's cross, and, therefore, bound by their professed relationship to pray for each other. "A Christian fellowship," he concluded, "lives and exists by the intercession of its members for one another, or it collapses. . . . Intercession is the purifying bath into which the individual and fellowship must enter every day. Intercession means nothing less than to bring our brother into the presence of God, to see him under the cross of Jesus as a poor human being and sinner in need of grace." [36]

Separated from his family and the visibly supportive fellowship of his Confessing Church while in prison, Bonhoeffer was consoled by the thought of his being remembered in the prayers offered on his behalf. Hence he once asked Bethge to promise that they "remain faithful in interceding for each other. . . . And if it should be decided that we are not to meet again, let us remember each other to the end in thankfulness and forgiveness, and may God grant us that one day we may stand before his throne praying for each other and joining in praise and thankfulness." [37] Their union in prayer was more than a mere leap of empathy. If Bonhoeffer was able to persevere in his prohuman freedom and anti-Hitler resolve, this was due in large part to the continual inspiration he derived from Bethge's friendship and prayerful support. "Please don't ever get anxious or worried about me, but don't forget to pray for me," he pleaded in one of his final letters; he then added, "I'm sure you don't! I am so sure of God's guiding hand that I hope I shall always be kept in that certainty. You must never doubt that I'm travelling with gratitude and cheerfulness along the road where I'm being led. My past life is brim-full of God's goodness, and my sins are covered by the forgiving love of Christ crucified." [38] In the strength of such a friendship and mutual prayer, his concern for personal survival and the safety of his loved ones yielded to the quiet confidence in God's protection that made his eventual death an act of faith and courageous resignation. Even as he attempted to cope with his own powerlessness over the fate awaiting him and his friends, he recognized that, "behind any anxiety . . . life has now been placed wholly in better and stronger hands." [39]

It was, indeed, this quiet confidence in God's protection which seems to permeate the prayers he composed for his fellow prisoners. Their constant theme is trust in God's love and acceptance of whatever God has willed. "Whatever this day may bring," he prayed, God's "name be praised." He commended into God's hands at close of day his loved ones and fellow prisoners, even the warders, as well as his own person. He asked for strength to bear what God sent and courage to overcome fear. In the all-pervasive distress of prison life, he would say to God: "I trust in your grace and commit my life wholly into your hands. Do with me according to your will and as is best for me. Whether I live or die, I am with you, and you, my God, are with me." [40] These prayers, which were circulated illegally among the cells, manifest many of the insights that helped guide Bonhoeffer's actions on behalf of peace and freedom and reveal his concern for Christian community and fellowship even in prison. In effect, Bonhoeffer was trying "to bring everyone in the sprawling prison of Tegel with whom he was able to make some kind of contact, by his own example, into the field of force from which he drew his own strength." [41]

He turned to God in his weakness, but he did not want his relationship with God to be limited to the outcry of pain and fear. As he declared in his letter of May 29, 1944, God "must be recognized at the center of life, not when we are at the end of our resources; it is his will to be recognized in life, and not only when death comes; in health and vigor, and not only in suffering; in our activities, and not only in sin." [42] God himself is the ground for this attitude, he tells us. The relationship in suffering is mutual. This is the ironical twist he gave to a poetical description of people going to God when they are desperate or in need of help, peace, bread, and mercy. Christians "go to God when he is sore bestead," and they find God "poor and scorned, without shelter or bread, whelmed under weight of the wicked, the weak, the dead; Christians stand by God in his hour of grieving." [43] People cannot only find God in their suffering; they are able to be a strength to him in his suffering in Christ. How God suffers and how God becomes weak are questions which must be pondered in the gospel story in which Christ identifies with the least of his brothers and sisters. Bonhoeffer saw himself in a way summoned to stand by God in the sufferings of his Christ in the person of Jews and all victims of Nazi aggression. His loss of freedom was part of "God's sufferings at the hands of a godless world." [44] God, in turn, gives hope and freedom in the whole mode of his human helplessness and in the trust in deliverance that becomes resurrection. Death itself loses something of its terror when, in God, it becomes the final step on the road to true freedom. [45]

These were prayers which further linked Bonhoeffer with the forceful, confident past of a long Christian tradition. Even though a prisoner, his life continued to be "a liturgy, praise from the depths, but in it and through it he was united to and supported by the voices in his ear." [46] We recognize in Bonhoeffer's spirituality the revered monastic discipline of daily prayers at fixed times of day and in moments of special celebration or stress. In his life in prison, as in his days of freedom in the Confessing Church, he followed the tempo of the church year and the pattern of liturgical feasts. These became the guidelines of his spirituality and the source of his consolation and courage in the forced separation from family and friends, as we see in so many references to the feasts and seasons in the prison letters. The structure of regular, rhythmical prayer would, he felt, enable people of faith to enter into the cadences of Christ's own life and to make of their whole lives a prayerful offering to God.[47]

It was to be expected, therefore, that in the illegal seminary of Finkenwalde, Bonhoeffer introduced his students to the structured life of prayer together that was to become the heart of their Christian community. He wanted to form their spirituality, like his, "according to the rhythm of the events in our Lord's own pilgrimage—advent, birth, epiphany, suffering and passion, crucifixion, resurrection, ascension, and parousia."[48] Bonhoeffer often led his seminarians in religious services, formulating prayers that gave thanks for their gift of faith and brotherhood and for the idyllic setting of their life together. He called for tolerance and forgiveness within the fellowship and intercession for the Confessing Church, the leaders of the church community, those in prison, and even enemies. Bethge reports that he gave "much time and trouble to the preparation of these prayers and their inner order. His language was wholly appropriate to the matter in hand and seemed completely free from all manifestations of self. Into these prayers he would put his will, his understanding, and his heart. Nevertheless, he believed that the language used in prayer should as a rule be modeled on that of the Psalms with which it should in any case harmonize."[49]

Bonhoeffer loved to pray the Psalms. They were Christ's prayer in him; they were Christ's prayer for his community. He called the Psalms a rich gift because they taught people "to pray as a fellowship."[50] The Psalms likewise lent themselves to the liturgical prayer of the Christian churches, because they seemed so well to express not only the moods of a community's relationship with God but also the turns of love and heartbreak, of joy and sorrow which are themselves the individual path to God. Christians must learn to speak with God "whether the heart is full or empty."[51] In the Psalms God shows people how they can experience with him, or, as Bonhoeffer claimed, how they can speak with God after the manner of Jesus himself. He pictures Christ in the Psalms as pouring out "the heart of all humanity before God," standing in our place and praying for us. The Psalms are the Christian's prayer because they are the prayer of Christ who "knows us better than we know ourselves." [52]

As one eager to enter entirely into the full life of a follower of Christ, Bonhoeffer put himself into a daily discipline of prayer nourished in moments of solitude and with readings from the Scriptures. One student of Bonhoeffer's spirituality has remarked from a perusal of his devotional guides in prison that he "began to realize with new appreciation the source of Bonhoeffer's spiritual stamina and vitality—his constant, daily, childlike relationship to God." [53] Indeed, this relationship is itself woven into the pattern of his daily prayer. There are no masks in Bonhoeffer's communion with God. His prayers are often poetic. But the beauty of his words comes not so much from the artistic quality of his poetry as from the grace of that relationship and the witness of his convictions in the loss of liberty and life that paradoxically became the way to freedom and deliverance.

Stations on the road to freedom: faith's liberating power

When the July 20 plot against Hitler collapsed in tactical failure and before his own situation in prison had further deteriorated, Bonhoeffer composed the poem which in so many ways retraces his life's journey, "Stations on the Road to Freedom." [54] Each "station" tells us of the nature of freedom and of the risk of faith. Freedom, he maintains, is born of the discipline of Christian discipleship. It is never to be mistaken for the uncontrolled venting of one's passions or the lack of mastery over one's "soul and senses." Freedom is never license to follow one's own whims or to retreat into the false security of indifference and sins of omission. Rather, the stern discipline of obedience to the Sermon on the Mount and to the Christ who accepted his Father's will unto death is the enigmatic path to true freedom. We see here traces of Bonhoeffer's dictum that only those who obey the concrete command of God can become followers of Christ in the costly grace of discipleship. In God's will lies the only way to experience true freedom.

But such freedom means also that a person be fully daring. It is only "through deeds, not through thoughts taking wing," (wishful thinking that evil will cease of itself without any effort on the part of Christians) that one can truly live in freedom. A church that could boast of its being a stronghold of sacramental power and spiritual liberation for people was, nonetheless, "in chains" unless it could take life-and-death risks on behalf of "the weakest and most defenseless brethren of Jesus Christ." [55] Bonhoeffer observed with both dismay and some bitterness the seeming conspiracy of inaction of churches and Christians, which gave respectability to the principles of Hitlerism and retarded active opposition to the horrors of the war and the death camps. The bland, churchy resolutions and pious prayers for peace may have saved only a sanctimonious front for the church, but few lives. The times called for brave deeds, even the scandal of treason, and a "shameful" plot to kill the evil dictator. Only the person who trusted deeply in God's love amid the "guilt" of those actions, repugnant to one's Christianity, could be free in the manner of Jesus. Only the person free to venture the paradoxical patriotism of treason could be truly Christian to the least of Christ's brothers and sisters, the innocent victims of racial hatred and the multitudes of suffering strewn in the ditches and rubble of a world war.

Bonhoeffer himself had crossed over the boundaries of law and respectability into an inner exile from churchly support and into the depressing world of imprisonment, interrogations, and threat of execution. In his poetry he described his hands, once "strong and active" in arousing the moral convictions of the conspirators and in negotiating the peace they had conspired for, as now "bound." "In helplessness," he saw that his actions against Nazism were ended. Yet he could still "sigh in relief," because his cause was committed "to stronger hands." The liberation of his nation was within his grasp, but he was allowed only to "draw near to touch freedom . . . ; then, that it might be perfected in glory, he gave it to God." Willingness to suffer for his personal commitment to Christ and for the deeds this faith elicited would be the most decisive step in Bonhoeffer's journey to the full experience of freedom. He sensed that God had called him to enter the fellowship of suffering, in which genuine faith would be tested in the extreme. Faith for him continued to be a "participation in the being of Jesus," whose life was one of utterly courageous service of people. He realized that this meant for him a being for others "maintained till death." [56] He had touched freedom in his decision to draw close to the freedom in suffering of Christ himself. It was now up to God to accept his willing sacrifice and to deliver him one way or another.

We see intimations of his realization that God was asking him for the supreme sacrifice of his life in two of his last communications with Bethge, the poems, "Jonah" and "The Death of Moses." Bonhoeffer's identification with these two biblical figures is obvious, though "Jonah" is a poem which could also have been written to and of the church, afraid to own up to its guilt and crying aloud "in fear of death." [57] Like Jonah, Bonhoeffer accepted his part in the guilt and disasters that had befallen his nation and church and offers his life to God. Bonhoeffer must himself sink beneath the waves of life along with his fellow conspirators. The death of Jonah will ultimately be salvific for the greater number of people.

The other poem, "The Death of Moses," is almost strangely prophetic of what did eventually happen to Bonhoeffer, although Germany of the postwar era could hardly be compared to the "promised land." Bonhoeffer depicted the aged Moses who has led his people to the edge of the promised land but who will not be allowed to enter that land himself. Moses can still thank God for all the blessings of "deliverance and salvation." He can even understand and accept his own death as punishment for the infidelity of his people. Moses could see the promised land in the distance and that in itself gives him joy. Others would live in the freedom he helped bring about by his sacrifice. In that act of resignation to God's will, Bonhoeffer has Moses say to God:

> Sinking, O God, into your eternities,
> I see my people enter into freedom.
> You who punish sin and gladly forgive,
> God, I have loved this people.
> That I carried their disgrace and their burdens,
> And I have seen their salvation—that is enough.[58]

Like the dying Moses and the crucified Christ, Bonhoeffer had already entered the path to the final and fullest experience of freedom. In his own death he would aspire to "cast aside all the burdensome chains." The hidden face of freedom he had sought in discipline, action, and suffering, he now recognized to be unveiled in his own death. Here alone would he experience that freedom that had been his life's personal quest, the freedom "revealed in the Lord." The only faith that could liberate the Christian was that lived in the shadow of the cross and in the strength of Christ's sacrifice. The full freedom for which he longed would be granted only in the seeming loss of all freedom in death. For the person of faith, however, dying for the sake of the gospel was to become resurrection, the beginning of life and the perfection of freedom. And so Bonhoeffer accepted his sentence with courage, because of the trust which had liberated him from fear of that final step. His death, in quiet confidence in the God who suffers, was for him the final liberation of faith.

6

Conclusion: Church, Bonhoeffer, and the Liberation of Peoples

South African theologian John De Gruchy told the story of an innocent question asked after Eberhard Bethge's lectures on Bonhoeffer in 1973. Some laymen who had attended one of Bethge's seminar sessions and who had no previous knowledge of Bonhoeffer wanted to know when Bonhoeffer had visited South Africa. "He knows our situation from the inside," one of them remarked.[1] The questioners had obviously missed mention of Bonhoeffer's death in 1945. Somehow Bonhoeffer's critique of the cozy relationship between church and state seemed perceptive and helpful. De Gruchy commented that few, indeed, in South Africa were familiar with Bonhoeffer's words and deeds. Though some claimed that in Europe and North America theology had moved "beyond Bonhoeffer," in South Africa, he noted, people had just begun to encounter his life and thought. De Gruchy's remarks seemed to echo Harvey Cox's assessment that the church will never move "beyond Bonhoeffer" until it "speaks with pointed specificity to its age" and "shapes its message and mission not for its own comfort but for the health and renewal of the world."[2]

"The view from below": a challenge to the churches

Whether the church is capable of inspiring or even leading this kind of renewal still remains a moot issue today. Will the church in these final decades of the 20th century be able to speak God's Word and do those courageous deeds that can even liberate a church from itself? Bonhoeffer argued that his own church was not only *not* free but, worse, was so interested in its own survival and in its own enjoyment of comfort that it became a sop to the powerful and belligerent. His theology took aim at the effete mediocrity that had made the church such an ineffective counterforce to the turbulent evil of a world trapped in genocidal war. The peace of 1945 was hardly a complete liberation of the church, if the continued pursuit of institutional self-aggrandizement is any measure of judging a church's professed dedication to the gospel. The "bourgeois church" hankering after the security of a guaranteed status quo and fearful of any prophetic voice that might threaten its peace is very much with us. The stated priorities of churches at local and international levels are often a witness to the manner in which religions can appear to serve only their own security needs or become preoccupied with trivia.

There is, indeed, a crisis of survival within the church today. This is not, as some parishes believe, the struggle of individual churches to ensure a sound financial base and to retain or even expand membership. Rather it is the age-old crisis of whether a church is truly the church of Jesus Christ. Or, as Bonhoeffer has put it, whether a church exists, like Christ, to be of service to others, even if this means unflinchingly to accept the "death" of its present forms and the denial of some of its less-than-central aims.

Bonhoeffer's theology constitutes an emphatic challenge to the churches to adopt as their own the prophetic freedom of Jesus and to strive for the achievement of human freedom wherever that struggle is joined. Bonhoeffer's personal participation in the conspirators' efforts to liberate their country from a morally destructive war went unsupported by the churches. On the contrary, church leaders, true to pietistic form, rushed to offer prayers of thanks for their Führer's astonishing escape from death in 1944. Bonhoeffer's imprisonment and execution were a lonely witness to where the church ought to have been: the 20th century's Golgotha of Nazi prisons and scaffolds.

That some churches have undertaken to accept this Christic challenge and the costly consequences of speaking the prophetic word and doing the more courageous deeds is likewise much in evidence today. More than ever before, churches appear to sense that evil is not a mere individual wrongdoing but may, in its most insidious form, be structured into the very makeup of society, both civil and ecclesial. This is a growing awareness on the part of the churches, reflected in the startling way church synods and conferences of church leaders have readily adopted resolutions affirming their identity with the oppressed people in those sections of the world called euphemistically the "underdeveloped nations" or the "Third World," or most recently, the "newly awakened peoples." It is further seen in the mounting vocal opposition of the churches to the nuclear arms race and to nations unleashing war in any form to solve their political and territorial squabbles. Finally, and perhaps most of all, this awareness is evident in the way the church has come to recognize that it has contributed to the problem. A vital part of Bonhoeffer's troubling legacy to the churches was his pointing out so tellingly the effects of careless church teaching and of the cowardly attitudes of ecclesial leaders. Christian churches, open to subversion by individuals and nations, became unwitting accomplices in the evil that will stand forever as the paradigm of 20th-century malevolence—the Holocaust.

This change in church attitudes toward the struggle for freedom is what Bonhoeffer perceived in the concluding paragraph of his essay gift to the conspirators, "After Ten Years": "We have for once learned to see the great events of world history from below, from the perspective of the outcast, the suspects, the maltreated, the powerless, the oppressed, the reviled—in short, from the perspective of those who suffer." [3] Bonhoeffer's own life was itself a steady journey from the comfort of a university teaching post to the bitterness of being a minority opposition to both church and state, from the safety of exile to the dangerous life of a conspirator, from clerical and familial privilege to the harsh imprisonment and death of a "traitor." This "view from below" was the perspective of a black preacher in Harlem, of a French pacifist, of pastors concerned about political idolatry creeping into their churches, of a fellow minister with Jewish blood, of inmates at Nazi prisons and death camps, of conspirators torn between loyalty to country and to conscience. The circumstances of his life helped Bonhoeffer to see the problems of his people from the view of "the oppressed." If there was a radical shift or "conversion" in his life, it was in that period when he rediscovered the Sermon on the Mount and realized that there were "things for which an uncompromising stand is worthwhile. And it seemed . . . that peace and social justice, or Christ himself are such things." [4]

Bonhoeffer and the Jews: church guilt in the Holocaust

In the era of the evil structured into national life and international belligerence by nazism, these issues of "peace and social justice, or Christ himself" seemed to converge on the "Jewish Question." While so much of Bonhoeffer's life and theology reveals a deep-set Christocentrism and an unwavering devotion to the Christian church, equally remarkable is his having identified so closely with the plight of those prime victims of Nazi hate, the Jews. This has several implications for the manner in which the Christian church still needs to be liberated from those prejudicial attitudes toward Judaism which tended to corrupt Christianity's identity almost from the very beginnings of church life. This is not the place to trace the history of Christian anti-

Semitism. Nor am I arguing that Bonhoeffer's heroic actions and sharp words on behalf of the Jews exculpate Christian churches from guilt in the Holocaust. On the contrary, there is as much a lesson to be learned from the fact that Bonhoeffer was so isolated and ultimately so ineffective in this cause as from his accusation that the Christian church was "guilty of the deaths of the weakest and most defenseless brothers of Jesus Christ." [5]

Part of that guilt is rooted in the hostility generated by Christianity's early and apparently bitter break with Judaism. The separation of Jews and Christians was more than a theological rift. Certainly Martin Buber, in his incisive way, has perceptively described the clash of vision that made the separation so inevitable: "To the Christian the Jew is the incomprehensibly obdurate man, who declines to see what has happened; and to the Jew the Christian is the incomprehensibly daring man who affirms in an unredeemed world that its redemption has been accomplished." [6] This is a gracious interpretation of a long history of invective and persecution in which Christians saw in Judaism a nagging reminder that the promise of Christianity was still unfulfilled and in Jews a convenient scapegoat for those societal ills that contradicted the promise. That hatred of Judaism constituted a clear rejection of Jesus, who joined compassion for the outcast with a spirit of peace and forgiveness, was a contradiction hardly noticed as Christian history became tainted with the quasi-religious sanctions that made repression of the Jews seem like virtuous, even "manly," action. The Jews were considered a people guilty of the death of Christ and, therefore, rejected by God and doomed to wander nationless at the mercy of peoples who would barely tolerate their presence among them.

When Bonhoeffer attempted to parry these pseudotheological rationalizations for the oppression and sufferings of the Jews, he encountered fierce opposition within his own church. He was reproved in his study of Ezra-Nehemiah, for example, for overlooking the issue of Jewish guilt in the murder of Jesus. As William Peck has observed: "Bonhoeffer did not hold any subgroup in the church or in world history responsible for Golgotha. Jesus was not simply a man, according to Bonhoeffer, but man—representative man. He was betrayed and killed by man, as much by the church of today as by the church of Ezra. This is Bonhoeffer's stand in opposition to the neutral theologians in a debate that leads from politics to the iconic-mythic issues of theology." [7] There is clearly a shift in Bonhoeffer's Bible studies during the 1930s in which he seemed at first to have interpreted everything from an extreme Christocentric typology and then ended by a respectful attempt to understand Christ himself from the vantage point of the Hebrew Scriptures. If in the beginning, and in keeping with Christian exegesis from the patristic period on, he could declare that the Old Testament belonged to Christ, by the time of his work in the conspiracy he could affirm that Christ belonged to the Jews. [8] Indeed, that he identified with them in the ghettos and death camps.

For Bonhoeffer it would not be sufficient absolution of guilt for the church to catalog those brave things Christians did to save Jews during World War II. Nor would it suffice to single out spirited vocal defenses of the Jews, even on the part of those, like Bonhoeffer, who would later give their lives. In Bonhoeffer's opinion, in this test of its vocation to be Christ to the world the church was guilty of being unfaithful. His bitterness against his church is evident in many of his writings, a bitterness stemming from what he sensed to be both a failure of trust in God and a denial of compassion. The brothers and sisters of Christians, he would insist to his seminarians, are not only those one encounters in explicitly Christian gatherings. Rather, Christ's closest brothers and sisters in suffering were the Jews, and the test of one's own Christian faith soon became whether one would speak up on behalf of these victims of Nazi racism. [9] He frequently cited Proverbs 31:8, "Open your mouth for those who have no voice" (auth. trans.), as the command which determined whether the church was "still the church of the present Christ." By this he meant one thing only: whether the church was opposed to the Aryan clause and prepared to be the Christ of the oppressed in the "Jewish Question." [10]

Such an extraordinary solidarity with the Jews on Bonhoeffer's part has been noted by Pinchas Lapide, who not only saw Bonhoeffer's theology of the 1930s take a surprisingly Judaic turn toward the Torah and the Mishnah but has also expressed this startling conclusion about where that theology might lead: "From a Jewish perspective Bonhoeffer is a pioneer and a forerunner of a slow step-by-step re-Hebraisation of the churches in our days." [11] Historian Ruth Zerner has carried this thought a step further in suggesting, along the lines of Bonhoeffer's "unconscious Christianity," that Bonhoeffer himself was an "unconscious Jew." This is somewhat evident in the way he refused to force the Jewish Scriptures and their rich traditions into Christian categories.[12] While Bonhoeffer's writings are hardly argument enough for a Christian return to Jewish roots, nonetheless they do offer a firmer base for the improvement of Jewish-Christian understanding in a world which must forever preserve the memories of Auschwitz. Bonhoeffer insists in his "Confession of Guilt" that the Jews are the brothers and sisters of Jesus Christ. No longer can a church assert, as even Bonhoeffer did in an earlier phase of his own defense of Jews, that the Jews have been displaced by Christians in God's plan of salvation, or that pogroms against Jews reflect their just punishment for rejecting the Christ, or that Christians have a mission to evangelize the Jews. These are the theological stereotypes which become hiding places for church leaders, while their less noetic, bullying minions seek out scapegoats for their own and a nation's misfortunes. Bonhoeffer argued the greater responsibility of those who egg on the violent mobs and of those who, by timidity or by indifference, make the mindless behavior of mobs possible. More than any other person, Bonhoeffer pointed out not only

that Christians must defend Jews but that the fate of Christians
was linked inexorably to the fate of Judaism:

> Western history is, by God's will, indissolubly linked with the
> people of Israel, not only in terms of origins, but also in a genuinely
> uninterrupted relationship. The Jew keeps open the question of
> Christ. He is the sign of God's free and merciful choice and of
> the repudiating wrath of God. "Behold therefore the goodness
> and severity of God" (Romans 11:22). An expulsion of the Jews
> from the West must necessarily bring with it the expulsion of
> Christ; for Jesus Christ was a Jew.[13]

These lines from Bonhoeffer's *Ethics* were composed at the
beginning of the deportations and before the official implemen-
tation of a policy of "final solution." The words are compelling,
but they are also a stark reminder to the Christian church that
to reject Judaism and the Jewish roots of Christianity is to reject
Christ himself. Bonhoeffer became a victim of the Holocaust in
solidarity with his Jewish brothers and sisters. It was to his
disappointment that the Christian church lacked the heart of
Christ himself and could still revel in the "cheap grace" of hom-
iletic platitude and self-justifying inaction. The church survived
only at the price of denying Christ anew.

Bonhoeffer's fate is a lesson for the Christian churches. If his
words have piqued the sensibilities of Christian officialdom,
even more have his deeds on behalf of those afflicted by the
evils of Nazism seemed to make him more squarely one with
Christ than those called to lead. The poignant memory of that
period of hypocrisy, apostasy, and ecclesial irresponsibility has
haunted the churches in present-day movements for liberation.
In the "Confession of Guilt," already alluded to, Bonhoeffer accused the churches of having "witnessed in silence the spoliation and exploitation of the poor and the enrichment and
corruption of the strong." He indicted the church for a silence
that rendered it "guilty of the decline in responsible action, in
bravery in the defense of a cause, and in willingness to suffer

for what is known to be right." [14] Today many of the churches are no longer silent. Nor do they appear to be lacking in courage. In fact, the Christian churches' growing identity with the cause of the poor and the dispossessed has been one of the most radical shifts in formal church policy in this century.

Bonhoeffer and contemporary liberation theology

The issues raised by Bonhoeffer's theology intersect current efforts by the churches to understand Christian mission not only in terms of the vocation to signify and proclaim salvation but also, in that proclamation, to affirm that salvation is inextricably linked to human liberation in all its forms. Evangelization proper proclaims the inherent worth of all peoples and refuses to tolerate the various forms of injustice that deny their dignity. The church believes it shares in the life and attitudes of Christ. An essential part of its mission, therefore, is to tell all Christians of the way the suffering Christ has assumed incarnate form in today's world. [15] If we are to search for that in Bonhoeffer which has set him as an inspirational figure in the budding liberation theology of our century, it would seem to be his deeply rooted, Christocentric belief in human dignity. In his day the denial of that dignity had assumed the grotesque shape of government by criminal and terroristic destruction of the basic freedoms that protected life and enhanced individuality. There is, unfortunately, a nazism of the heart perduring in modern dictatorships, which, under the guise of preserving political order and economic stability, stifle freedom of speech and perpetuate socioeconomic subservience. Church leaders are aware, as many never were during the Hitler tyranny, that structures of enslavement, whether from the political left or right, are hostile to the gospel. Not to counteract this evil is to renounce the mission of being Christ's presence in the world, proclaiming, as he did, hope for the release of captive peoples.

This is precisely the biting edge of Bonhoeffer's critique of church acquiescence to the will of highly structured, militarily aggressive, and utterly ruthless political powers. Bonhoeffer's theology goads the churches to abandon their flight from the world into the safe haven of religiosity and sacramentality. Today's liberation theology also encourages the church to accept responsibility for the course of history, even if it means confrontation with the political realm. Religion need not be, as Marx thought, a social narcotic for the masses—nor may churches invoke God-given orders of either nature or preservation to push people meekly to accept societal evil as if some extraterrestrial force had decreed it. Bonhoeffer argued that it is always human agency, not a divinely protected state order, that is responsible for the violation of humanity and the corruption of a whole society.

This conviction led him to begin a social ethic he would never finish but whose direction for the church was obvious. He held the church accountable for the way history is shaped by nations. The most pressing question for him, then, is not how to escape sinless from the imperative to oppose state policies or even to overthrow the state, but how one should enter the struggle for the sake of the coming generation whose very humanity is threatened.[16]

As we have seen, it was only with difficulty that Bonhoeffer was able to steer his thinking beyond the Lutheran heritage, which affirmed clear boundaries between "gospel and sword" and a mutuality of purpose in God's order for both church and state. Such a traditional separation seemed to protect the state from any church interference and vice-versa. Bonhoeffer, on the contrary, asserted that while the church could not identify with any particular political order however Christian, nonetheless "it can and must oppose every concrete order which constitutes an offense to faith in Jesus Christ."[17] In the name of such opposition the church, he noted as early as 1933, could be involved in "direct political action" when the state has failed in its duty to maintain law and order.[18] It is obvious that the Nazi vision of law and order was hardly congruent with Bonhoeffer's espousal of the freedom to resist unjust laws and an idolatrous order. For Bonhoeffer involvement in the penultimate cause of preserving what is necessary for human rights became the only adequate way to "prepare the way of the Lord." [19]

Though these penultimate values may be as mundane as the basic needs of food, shelter, education, and medical care, with which people are enabled to live with dignity, they may also involve open conflict for the demarginalization of those who have no governmental voice against measures that are exploitive, enslaving, or merely demeaning. In the "Movement of Church and Society in Latin America" (ISAL), for example, Bonhoeffer's manner of promoting Christian involvement in action to achieve those penultimate goals showed a way beyond the impasse of competing ideologies in what often becomes a class struggle. That way for Bonhoeffer was the *deed* which in some way pointed to Christ himself.

In the current endeavor to liberate peoples, both Christians and Marxists seem to have discovered common ground. Julio de Santa Ana has remarked on this phenomenon that the ISAL movement resolved the possible conflict of aims and ideologies by appeal to Bonhoeffer's rejection of both radicalism and compromise in favor of a Christian ethic in which Christ's incarnation, death, and resurrection give a balanced direction to one's social energies. Bonhoeffer wrote:

> Radicalism hates patience, and compromise hates decision. Radicalism hates wisdom, and compromise hates simplicity. Radicalism hates moderation and measure, and compromise hates the immeasurable. Radicalism hates the real, and compromise hates the word. To contrast the two attitudes in this way is to make it sufficiently clear that both alike are opposed to Christ. For in Jesus Christ those things which are here ranged in mutual hostility are one. . . . In Jesus Christ we have faith in the incarnate, crucified and risen God. In the incarnation we learn of the love of God for

his creation; in the crucifixion we learn of the judgment of God upon all flesh; and in the resurrection we learn of God's will for a new world. There could be no greater error than to tear these three elements apart; for together they comprise the whole.[20]

Adoption of this attitude enabled the ISAL to enter into cooperative ventures with Marxists while accepting neither the Marxist ideology, which defined itself as atheist, nor the "Christian" ideology, which justified oppression simply because its exponents used the name "Christian" in identifying their government or belonged to Christian denominations. The ISAL could, therefore, share in the aims of a Marxist ideology if that meant cooperation in programs of social justice and the end of intolerance and Gestapo-like oppression. For them, the humanization sought was rooted in the demands of human dignity and the equally resonant demands of Christ who had himself identified with the hungry, the homeless, the lonely, the imprisoned, and the enslaved. This is not the ultimate, but the effort to rectify injustice does, as Bonhoeffer has argued, pertain necessarily to that ultimate. From this it has also followed that, in the name of the gospel, Christians must criticize, even denounce and openly combat, the power groups that deny people their basic rights and crowd them into narrow corners of human pathos, thereby denying them a chance to recognize God in the midst of a life more richly human.

Christian cooperation with Marxists in freedom movements and in terms of some common humanistic goals has grown along with overcoming the mentality that has kept the church so rigidly separate from the world and hindered active involvement of the church in matters deemed overtly secular. In countries where economic oppression and exploitation of lower classes are often spearheaded by "respectable" churchgoers and legitimated by religion in its avidity for law and order, there is an even stronger need for the church to be, as Bonhoeffer had urged, a hub of intelligent discussion of problems, of contro-

versy, and of concern for people.[21] Bonhoeffer realized that ecclesial thinking in two disconnected spheres—natural versus
supernatural, profane versus sacred, world versus church—had
become a convenient ghetto in which one could find spiritual
security in a flight from responsible action. In declaring that the
world had come of age and could solve most problems without
the so-called God hypothesis, Bonhoeffer was asking the church
to enter into the full throes of "living completely in this world."
Action for others by the church had to be genuinely humanistic,
in the sense that the church would "share in the secular problems of ordinary human life, not dominating, but helping and
serving. It must tell people of every calling what it means to
live in Christ, to exist for others." [22]

For those engaged in today's struggle for the liberation of
peoples this has meant that churches must step beyond their
old, comfortable frontiers, where action on behalf of justice was
limited to the bluster of inoffensive platitudes. Christians have
been urged to take a critical part in the full cultural, economic,
and political life of their nations when such involvement can
lead to a new advent of justice. In South and Central America
this has meant for some a liberation from the paradigm of the
American way of life or of the American dream come commer-
cially true. For others, this has entailed a sobering rejection of
many values and laws imposed by the ruling oligarchies and
supported by the politics of their church affiliation. In a world
shredded by ideology and class struggle a gradual liberation of
conscience has taken place. Within the churches this liberation
has assumed the form of an awakening to the real nature of their
mission to the world and a more realistic assessment of the
sources of injustice in society.

Church solidarity with the oppressed

There has been in recent years a growing eagerness of the
churches to align themselves with the oppressed, evident in

church documents of both Catholic and Protestant denominations. In many cases this shift has been made possible by a gradual abandonment of the "thinking in two spheres" mentality, which in earlier times had helped the church resolve the dilemma of whether the church's mission was totally "spiritual," directed to the salvation of souls, or also directed to the achievement of humanistic goals that would promote a better quality of life. The price of concentrating solely on the "spiritual" was often an aloofness from the common people in struggles for liberation. Yet the implications of integrating the defense of and agitation for human rights into the church's mission of evangelization have also appeared frightening to churches which see themselves forced into taking stands offensive to some of the so-called "faithful" (often the most affluent). The church could not, in such instances, be all things to all people, especially if some of the people could threaten a church's financial base. Though "compromise" seemed the more diplomatic route, this was the very tactic Bonhoeffer had denounced within the World Alliance of Churches, desperately posturing to be "diplomatic," and within his own German church, cowed by the threat of economic deprivation and personal incarceration.

For the Catholic church it has, indeed, been a long road from Pope Pius XI's declaration that "the objective of the Church is to evangelize, not to civilize. If it civilizes, it is for the sake of evangelization." [23] Or even Vatican II's teaching: "Christ, to be sure, gave his Church no proper mission in the political, economic, or social order. The purpose he set before her is a religious one." [24] That Vatican II's words on the issue represent a compromise is evident when one notes that standing out in even bolder relief is the following injunction:

> For the rest, the right to have a share of earthly goods sufficient for oneself and one's family belongs to everyone. The Fathers and Doctors of the Church held this view, teaching that men are obliged to come to the relief of the poor and to do so not merely

out of their superfluous goods. If a person is in extreme necessity, he has the right to take from the riches of others what he himself needs. . . . According to their ability, let all individuals and governments undertake a genuine sharing of their goods.[25]

Eleven years later, the Pontifical Commission on Justice and Peace noted that "the Church as a whole, like every Christian community, is called to work for the dignity and rights of man, both individually and collectively; to protect and promote the dignity of the human person; and to denounce and oppose every sort of human oppression." [26]

In the areas of the world which are the main concern of liberation theology, the change toward direct church action on behalf of political-economic justice is often traced back to the Conference of Latin American Bishops in Medellin in 1968 and the Conference of Christians for Socialism in Santiago, Chile, in 1972, in which the church moved from denunciation of injustice to a call to all "to defend the rights of the oppressed." [27] Though peaceful solutions are obviously to be preferred to violence, the Bishops have come to grips in these documents with the same dilemma Bonhoeffer faced in the 1930s. When political powers ignore the cry of the oppressed, they are themselves guilty of a violence of indifference, if not of deeds, and are thereby edging their own people to rebellion.

Within the Protestant tradition the World Council of Churches has moved toward similar support of those whose human rights have been infringed by military dictatorships and the powerful, greedy oligarchies that control most of a nation's wealth. The conference of the Church and Society Commission of the World Council of Churches held in Geneva in 1966 was as much a watershed for Protestant churches and the Third World as Medellin was for the Latin American Bishops. The call for a "responsible society" by the first postwar assembly of the WCC in 1948 was echoed in Geneva by recognition that such "responsibility" may include revolutionary violence, which is a counteraction to that "violence which, though bloodless, condemns whole populations to perennial despair." Nonetheless, in an attempt to show the terrible ambiguity of the violence it appeared to sanction, the conference also urged Christians to "think of the day after the revolution, when justice must be established by clear minds and in good conscience. There is no virtue in violence itself, but only in what will come after it." [28]

Liberation and the criteria for violence

This caution is important particularly for those who have joined movements of liberation for the sake of the gospel. Those who look on themselves as proponents of liberation theology, though they may bear the same weapons as their Marxist-atheist counterparts, are as aware of Jesus' legacy of forgiveness and peace as of Hannah Arendt's pungent observation that revolutionaries end up by devouring their own children. Violence should not be romanticized. Nor should armed revolution to achieve social justice be followed by an equally brutal vengeance directed against so-called enemies of the people. Bonhoeffer appeals to Third World revolutionaries, it is true, but it would be a wrong assessment of his life or theology to use him to justify any and all violence in the just cause. For him, violence was only an extreme measure when peaceful solutions were impossible; it was an abandonment of the Christian pacifism he preferred, and it was to be deplored. Always a resort to physical force could be contemplated only in the *ultima ratio*, or last resort, that extreme necessity when those "afflicted beyond endurance" can achieve redress by no other means. One did not seek to justify violence. On the contrary, the conspirators, driven to the responsible deed that is so admired in the post-Nazi era, were plunged in that guilt which only Christ could assume unto himself and only God could absolve. Violence was never the norm.

According to Bonhoeffer, one had always to allow the projected consequences of action on both the affected peoples and the coming generation to dictate a sense of reality in planning the overthrow of a tyranny. Adoption of extreme forms of resistance to the state became subject, then, to definite criteria. There had to be evidence of gross misconduct and no foreseeable exercise of responsibility by those responsible for the correct conduct of a state. Even with this, Bonhoeffer's awareness of the potentially brutal retaliation by authorities after a failed coup led him to postulate that the plot must have some promise of success. Paradoxically, and this was itself a factor in the technical failure of the July 20, 1944, plot, only a minimum of force could be applied. Finally, the action itself had to be taken as a last resort.[29]

No one would argue that these guidelines of Bonhoeffer for armed resistance to the Nazi state are those adopted by today's liberationists. There are, at the same time, unmistakable parallels between Bonhoeffer's ethics of resistance, however lacking in clear norms, and the ethics advocated by liberation theology. Bonhoeffer's "guidelines" are a bracing reminder that while Bonhoeffer is an inspiration to the liberation movement of today, his actions and writings in the anti-Hitler conspiracy should never be shuffled around as an argument for revolutionary violence of all sorts, even against a particularly oppressive regime and in an obviously just cause.[30]

The cross of Christ: symbol of courage in faith

In today's freedom movements Bonhoeffer offers no easy solutions to the problems besetting revolutionaries or the church. During the period of his *The Cost of Discipleship* he had inveighed against settling for "cheap grace," which could take on such a variety of enticing religious shapes. These were especially the religiosity or false piety whereby Christians could evade the more demanding problem of how to be faithful to Christ in the

ambiguity of conflicting visions and tactics. Killing the oppres-
sors in the name of justice could be as cheap a solution as the
less risky decision to do nothing while God, state, and nature
ran their course.

Third World theologians, like Julio de Santa Ana, as indeed
those involved in the struggle to be free within that troubled
sphere, have drawn much inspiration from Bonhoeffer's heroic
role in the German resistance to nazism. In studying Bonhoeffer
they have also been confronted with his equally strong opposition to war and fanaticism, to church apathy as well as trium-
phalism, and to the tendency both to glorify violence and to
avoid responsibility for action by a vapid appeal to Christ's teach-
ings wrenched out of any social context. This is a Bonhoeffer
attracted to Gandhi's nonviolence but revolted by nazism's total
lack of compassion and conscience.

Bonhoeffer offers not only an example of responsibility for
decisive action but also of the courage in faith inspired by
Christ's life and death for others. Indeed, it was the cross of
Christ, symbol both of a criminal's fate and a Savior's destiny,
of death in loneliness and of hope in desperation, which guided
Bonhoeffer into those deeds which would cost him his life. Bonhoeffer's example has helped clarify the question of conscience
for those engaged in the struggle for liberation. Following Christ
in these conflicts will inevitably cost Christians and church dear-
ly; for Bonhoeffer the cross is the price of "costly grace." A
privileged church is called to shed its privileges and affluence.
A fearful church is cautioned to seek its freedom, not in the
protection of and as gift from a powerful state, but only from
the gospel.[31] This will be a paradoxical freedom, akin to that
experienced by Christ himself even in the bleakest moments of
his being handed over to the "powers of darkness." The church
is challenged by Bonhoeffer's theology to be free enough to
offend the power brokers of this world on behalf of the weak
and helpless victimized by power. Bonhoeffer emphasized this

point in a London sermon at the height of Hitler's popularity: "Christendom adjusted itself far too easily to the worship of power. Christians should give much more offence; they should shock the world far more than they are now doing. Christians should take a stronger stand in favor of the weak rather than ponder the possible right of the strong." [32]

It is Bonhoeffer's legacy to the churches that they are reminded of Christ's mandate to set their ministry in the midst of the suffering world. The church is the church, he has insisted, only when it exists for others. This means a church willing to suffer for those who would otherwise be without a voice and defenseless. The Christian message of God's love for the world is only a hollow blare if the church's credibility is not grounded in its solidarity with oppressed peoples and in its willingness even to die for those it would deliver from evil. Bonhoeffer's *Ethics* contain the remarkable claim that "it is with the Christ who is persecuted and who suffers in his church that justice, truth, humanity and freedom now seek refuge." [33] It is Bonhoeffer's enduring significance to the church and contemporary society that in the most seductive threat to Christian faith in our century he was one with the Christ who suffers in all the victims of politically and militarily structured oppression.

Notes

Abbreviations Used

Books by Bonhoeffer

SC   *Sanctorum Communio*, trans. Ronald G. Smith et al. (London: Collins, 1963); published in the United States as *The Communion of Saints* (New York: Harper & Row, 1963).

AB   *Act and Being*, trans. Bernard Noble (New York: Harper & Row, 1962).

CF   *Creation and Fall*, trans. Kathleen Downham (New York: Macmillan, 1966).

CC   *Christ the Center*, trans. John Bowden (New York: Harper & Row, 1966).

GS   *Gesammelte Schriften*, 1 (1958) to 6 (1974), all published by Kaiser Verlag in Munich. Translations of parts of these volumes are contained in *NRS, WF,* and *TP* (see below).

NRS   *No Rusty Swords: Letters, Lectures and Notes, 1928-1936,* from the *Collected Works of Dietrich Bonhoeffer,* vol. 1, ed. Edwin H. Robertson, trans. Edwin H. Robertson and John Bowden (New York: Harper & Row, 1965).

WF   *The Way to Freedom: Letters, Lectures and Notes, 1935-1939,* from the *Collected Works of Dietrich Bonhoeffer,* vol. 2, ed. Edwin H. Robertson, trans. Edwin H. Robertson and John Bowden (New York: Harper & Row, 1966).

TP   *True Patriotism: Letters, Lectures and Notes, 1939-1945,* from the *Collected Works of Dietrich Bonhoeffer,* vol. 3, ed. Edwin H. Robertson, trans. Edwin H. Robertson and John Bowden (New York: Harper & Row, 1973).

CD   *The Cost of Discipleship,* trans. R.H. Fuller, rev. by Irmgard Booth (New York: Macmillan, 1966).

LT   *Life Together,* trans. John W. Doberstein (New York: Harper & Row, 1954).

E   *Ethics,* trans. Neville Horton Smith (New York: Macmillan, 1965).

LPP   *Letters and Papers from Prison,* trans. Reginald H. Fuller, 4th ed., trans. of additional material by John Bowden (New York: Macmillan, 1972).

WK   *Das Wesen der Kirche,* ed. Otto Dudzus (Munich: Chr. Kaiser Verlag, 1971).

PFP   *Prayers from Prison,* interpreted by Johann Christoph Hampe (Philadelphia: Fortress Press, 1979).

Secondary Literature

DB   Eberhard Bethge, *Dietrich Bonhoeffer: Theologian, Christian, Contemporary,* trans. Eric Mosbacher, Peter and Betty Ross, Frank Clarke, and William Glen-Doepel, ed. Edwin H. Robertson (New York: Harper & Row, 1970).

BEM   Eberhard Bethge, *Bonhoeffer: Exile and Martyr,* edited and with an essay by John W. de Gruchy (New York: Seabury, 1975).

IKDB   Wolf-Dieter Zimmermann and Ronald Gregor Smith, eds. *I Knew Dietrich Bonhoeffer: Reminiscences by His Friends,* trans. Käthe Gregor Smith (New York: Harper & Row, 1966).

SCH   Clifford J. Green, *The Sociality of Christ and Humanity: Dietrich Bonhoeffer's Early Theology,* 1927-1933 (Missoula, Montana: Scholars Press, 1975).

USQR   *Union Seminary Quarterly Review*

MW   *Die Mündige Welt,* I-V, ed. Eberhard Bethge et al. (Munich: Chr. Kaiser Verlag, 1955-1969).

Preface

1. *CD*, 44. In my later research I discovered that the original German has the expression "ravens" (*die Raben*) for "eagles." When I refer to this passage in my talks on Bonhoeffer, I usually manage to substitute "Christians" for "Lutherans," in order to make the force of Bonhoeffer's words applicable to more than just the Lutheran churches.

Chapter 1

1. Cited in George K.A. Bell, "The Church and the Resistance Movement," *IKDB*, 209-210.
2. *DB*, 22-23.
3. *DB*, 22.
4. Dietrich's choice of career may well have been more deeply motivated by the desire to accomplish something unique in a family of achievers. Undoubtedly, there was much personal ambition and vanity packed into his decision to become a theologian and thus to compete with his scientific-agnostic older brothers and father. Later he would express regret that he had entered the world of academe for less than Christian motives. Cf. Clifford Green, *SCH*, 174-175.
5. Cited in John Godsey, *The Theology of Dietrich Bonhoeffer* (Philadelphia: Westminster, 1960), 21. See also the tribute paid Bonhoeffer by Barth in the *Church Dogmatics*, 4, 2, where Barth writes: "If there can be any possible vindication of Reinhold Seeberg, it is to be sought in the fact that his school could give rise to this man and this dissertation, which not only awakens respect for the breadth and depth of its insight as we look back to the existing situation, but makes far more instructive and stimulating and illuminating and genuinely edifying reading today than many of the more famous works which have since been written on this problem of the Church .... I openly confess that I have misgivings whether I can even maintain the high level reached by Bonhoeffer saying no less in my own words and context, and saying it no less forcefully, than did this young man so many years ago" (641).
6. *SC*, 101 *et passim.*
7. *AB*, 90.
8. Historian Ruth Zerner has included many important details of Bonhoeffer's friendship with Frank Fisher and its influence on his theology in her article, "Dietrich Bonhoeffer's American Experiences: People, Letters, and Papers from Union Seminary," *USQR*, 31, 4 (Summer 1976), 266-275. On the influence of Jean Lasserre on Bonhoeffer's theology, see my article, "An Interview with Jean Lasserre," *USQR*, 27, 3 (Spring 1972), 149-160.
9. *DB*, 155.
10. Letter of February 26, 1932, *NRS*, 150-151.
11. Richard Rother, "A Confirmation Class in Wedding," *IKDB*, 57.
12. See *DB*, 146ff.

13. See Bonhoeffer's paper, "A Theological Basis for the World Alliance?" delivered at the Youth Peace Conference in Czechoslovakia July 26, 1932, *NRS*, 162-163.
14. "The Leader and the Individual in the Younger Generation," *NRS*, 202.
15. Cited in E.H. Robertson, *Christians Against Hitler* (London: SCM Press, 1962), 25-26. Even more frightening was the crude bit of prose taught in the schools: "As Jesus set men free from sin and hell, so Hitler rescued the German people from destruction. Both Jesus and Hitler were persecuted; but while Jesus was crucified, Hitler was exalted to Chancellor. While the disciples of Jesus betrayed their master and left him in his distress, the 16 friends of Hitler stood by him. The Apostles completed the work of their Lord. We hope that Hitler may lead his work to completion. Jesus built for heaven: Hitler, for the German earth" (ibid., p.18).
16. Ibid., 50 (translation slightly altered). For the complete text of Barmen's declarations, resolutions, and motions, see Arthur C. Cochrane, *The Church's Confession under Hitler* (Pittsburgh: Pickwick Press, 1976), 237-247.
17. So called because many of the ministers showed up wearing their brown uniforms and making the scene look like a "paramilitary spectacle." See *DB*, 237ff.
18. Letter of November 20, 1933, *NRS*, 237-240.
19. *DB*, 468; see also *BEM*, 88-89. Earlier Bonhoeffer had expressed his impatience with the Alliance's irresoluteness in a letter to Pastor Henriod, Secretary to the World Alliance in Geneva. In this letter, he wrote: "The slowness of ecumenical procedure is beginning to look to me like irresponsibility. A decision has got to be taken some time, and it's no good waiting indefinitely for a sign from heaven that will solve the difficulty without further trouble. Even the ecumenical movement has to make up its mind and is therefore subject to error, like everything human. But to procrastinate and prevaricate simply because you're afraid of erring, just when others—I mean our brethren in Germany—are daily having to come to infinitely difficult decisions seems to me almost to be going counter to love. To delay or fail to make decisions may be more sinful than to make wrong decisions out of faith and love" (*DB*, 294).
20. *DB*, 454-469.
21. On the significance of Bonhoeffer's interest in India, see William J. Peck, "The Significance of Bonhoeffer's Interest in India," *Harvard Theological Review*, 61 (July 1968), 431-450.
22. See *DB*, 346-387; also *IKDB*, 107ff.
23. *DB*, 385.
24. *TP*, 166 (trans. from *GS*, 2, 584 slightly altered).
25. *DB*, 155.
26. *CD*, 36 *et passim*.
27. *GS*, 1, 320; *DB*, 559.
28. *LPP*, 279.

29. *LPP*, 342.
30. *DB*, 823.
31. Sigismund Payne Best, *The Venlo Incident* (London: Hutchinson, 1950), 200.
32. *DB*, 830.
33. *DB*, 830; also *IKDB*, 232.

Chapter 2

1. Harvey Cox has suggested that, "like those indistinct ink blots in a Rorschach test, Dietrich Bonhoeffer's equivocal theological residue elicits wildly different interpretations. . . . Deciphering Bonhoeffer has become a wide-open pastime. . . ." See Harvey Cox, "Using and Misusing Bonhoeffer," *Christianity and Crisis*, 24 (October 19, 1964), 199.
2. See "The Religious Experience of Grace and the Ethical Life," *GS*, 3, 96, where Bonhoeffer stated: "Christian thinking admits that it thinks in circles, because it thinks with the premise that God really has revealed himself in Christ and that this revelation is the only truth; but it insists that all thinking about truth must think in a circle, because it presumes what it is going to prove. It is obvious that thinking which does not reside in truth cannot think truth. That is the general philosophical form of the Christian claim."
3. These are the opening words of Bonhoeffer's unpublished seminar paper, *"Lässt sich eine historische.und pneumatische Auslegung der Schrift unterscheiden, und wie stellt sich die Dogmatik hierzu?"* ("Can a Distinction Be Drawn between a Historical and a Pneumatological Interpretation of the Scriptures, and What Is the Attitude of Dogmatic Theology toward this?").
4. Peter Berger, with exaggeration, has detected in this somewhat of a "dogmatic imperialism." See his "Sociology and Ecclesiology," in Martin E. Marty, ed., *The Place of Bonhoeffer* (New York: Association Press, 1962), 60.
5. Clifford Green has shown conclusively that Bonhoeffer's theology of sociality is the context for his ecclesiology. See *SCH*, 55ff.
6. *SC*, 81-82.
7. *SC*, 107. On the implications of Christ's reconciling action for a theology of revelation, see my article, "Revelation in Christ: A Study of Bonhoeffer's Theology of Revelation," *Ephemerides Theologicae Lovanienses*, 50, 1 (May 1974), 43-44.
8. On the various meanings of *Stellvertreter*, see John Godsey, "Reading Bonhoeffer in English Translation: Some Difficulties," *USQR*, 23, 1 (Fall 1967), 84.
9. *SC*, 112 (trans. slightly altered).
10. *SC*, 123 (trans. slightly altered).
11. *SC*, 101.
12. *SCH*, 107.
13. *SCH*, 110.

14. *AB*, 32, 47.
15. *AB*, 121 (trans. from *SCH*, 119).
16. *AB*, 90-91.
17. *AB*, 124 (trans. from *SCH*, 122-123).
18. *CC*, 102.
19. *CC*, 34-37.
20. *CC*, 91.
21. *CC*, 43.
22. *CC*, 45.
23. *CC*, 46.
24. *CC*, 47. Bonhoeffer's statement here, as also his entire *pro me* (God's existence on behalf of his creatures) theology, was drawn from Luther, who had written: "So it is one thing if God is there, and another if he is there for you" (*Weimar Ausgabe*, 23, 150, 13, Kritische Gesammtausgabe, eds. J. K. F. Knaake et al., 1883).
25. *CC*, 48.
26. *CC*, 48-49.
27. *CC*, 51.
28. *CC*, 31.
29. *CC*, 59.
30. *CD*, 29.
31. *CD*, 36-37.
32. *CD*, 49.
33. *CD*, 154.
34. *CD*, 84.
35. *CD*, 85.
36. *CD*, 87.
37. *CD*, 269.
38. *CC*, 63-65.
39. *E*, 198.
40. *E*, 229. For a comparison of the thought of Bonhoeffer and Teilhard de Chardin, see Charles M. Hegarty, "Bonhoeffer and Teilhard: Christian Prophets of Secular Sanctity," *The Catholic World*, April 1968, 31-34; also his "Bonhoeffer and Teilhard on Worldly Christianity," *Science et Esprit*, 21, 1 (1969), 35-70.
41. *E*, 229-230.
42. *LPP*, 279.
43. See *CC*, 116-117.
44. This is, to be more exact, a general stress discernible in the letters. Bonhoeffer was careful to maintain the dialectic crucifixion-resurrection, as is evident from an examination of *LPP*, 240, 299, 336.
45. *LPP*, 336.
46. Letter of June 27, 1944, *LPP*, 337.
47. *LPP*, 381-382.

48. See *AB*, 90. In discussing the entire question of freedom in his commentary on Genesis, Bonhoeffer had insisted that this was a *relational* rather than an individualistic concept. "Only in relationship with the other am I free. No substantial or individualistic concept of freedom can conceive of freedom ... it is the message of the Gospel that God's freedom has bound us to itself, that his free grace only becomes real in this relation to us, and that God does not will to be free for himself but for man. God in Christ is free for man. Because he does not retain his freedom for himself the concept of freedom only exists as 'being free for' " (*CF*, 37). This freedom is a decisive element in the *pro me* structure of Bonhoeffer's theology. In the Berlin Christology lectures, for example, he stated: "He [Christ] is the one who has really bound himself to me in free existence. And he is the one who has freely preserved his contingency in his 'being-there for you'" (*CC*, 48).

Chapter 3

1. *LPP*, 370-372.
2. *LPP*, 217-218 (emphasis mine). "Resistance and Submission" (*Widerstand und Ergebung*) is the title Eberhard Bethge gave to the German publication of the letters.
3. "Concerning the Christian Idea of God," *GS*, 3, 102 (emphasis mine). It is important to Bonhoeffer that faith be considered a *direct* act in which a person turns toward God in Jesus Christ. This alone is, for him, the faith which justifies. As we will see later, he insisted on the directness of the act of faith in order to avoid identifying faith with either reflection or preaching or, worse still, systems which masquerade as faith.
4. See *AB*, 47; also *GS*, 3, 102-103.
5. *DB*, 154-155.
6. Letter to Erwin Sutz of February 26, 1932, cited in *DB*, 154.
7. *SCH*, 106-112.
8. *SCH*, 107.
9. *AB*, 71-72.
10. *SCH*, 112.
11. *AB*, 28.
12. *AB*, 31.
13. *AB*, 90-91.
14. *AB*, 119ff.
15. *AB*, 121.
16. *SCH*, 120.
17. *AB*, 124 (trans. slightly altered).
18. *AB*, 159-160.
19. *AB*, 141. Bonhoeffer distinguished between faith (*Glaube*) and wishful belief (*Gläubigkeit*). Although he admits that every act of faith is "wishful"

in the sense of being bound up in a person's psyche and, therefore, accessible to human reflection in some way, nevertheless, he insists that true faith is essentially the active intentionality toward Christ having as its base a person's being in the community of Christ. See *AB, 175.*

20. Letter of April 8, 1936, *DB*, 156. Bethge adds that, "Bonhoeffer never revealed the biographical background of these ideas to his students. They knew nothing of any inner revolution that took place at any particular time. Bonhoeffer always greatly disliked stories of conversion told by pietists for purposes of edification. But that did not cause him to shrink back from decisions that had matured in his mind which could become the foundation for a new future, including a new sense of responsibility for the world in his last years."

21. *AB*, 147-148.

22. *AB*, 148-151.

23. This is a consistent theme in Bonhoeffer's theology. Man "in Adam" is prone to the evil of self-isolation and self-glorification. He lives the "untruth" that he can do without others. In his hubris he breaks with the community only to end up in the "dreadful loneliness of an echo-less solitude." *CF*, 90. See also *CD*, 338.

24. *AB*, 155-162; 175-176. If we agree with Bonhoeffer that faith cannot be identified with reflection on the self, we can, nevertheless, investigate the possibility that genuine faith can and must include reflection on itself and on the self, or even, as Tillich has insisted, radical doubt. If faith is to produce a radical change in one's perspective, characterized by Bonhoeffer as a totally Christocentric outlook, we may legitimately ask how this is possible without admitting a thoroughgoing reflection on oneself into the whole process of faith. By this we do not mean narcissistic introspection, which Bonhoeffer has rightly condemned, but a faith in which the thinking subject may reflect on himself and his faith in terms of the radical impact Christ has made on his life. Understandably, Bonhoeffer doesn't want to place faith under the control of the thinking-reflecting "I." Yet if the revelation that provokes faith is bound up into the total complexity of human life and history, then it would make sense that God relates to a person not simply in moving him into communion with Christ in faith but also in the whole thinking-intuiting-reflecting process whereby people may accept God's grace and actively commit themselves to the "new life." This is not incompatible with "reflection" on the human possibilities and limitations to which God's historical revelation in Christ is addressed. Faith must be congruent with a person's deepest sense of reality and of the intelligible in experience. If revelation comes to expression in the religious symbols and language inspirited by faith, then these, in turn, should mirror the point of intersection where God's Word reaches human intelligibility, namely, in its concrete conjunction with the ordinary life of the believer. To separate reflection on faith and the self from faith itself, even for theological purposes, is to weaken the meaningfulness, even necessity, for faith

of symbolic-linguistic descriptions of the God who reveals himself in Christ as being in relationship with the self. The process of revelation should, therefore, include not only the "Word" event of faith but also all the human contours of the consequent God-human relationship as it extends into the everyday sacred-secular activity of the believer. A profound awareness of the human, which is opened up by a deep reflection on the self, together with an other-centered perspective, such as Bonhoeffer suggested in calling Jesus "the man for others," is an integral aspect of adult faith.

25. *AB*, 92.
26. *LPP*, 382.
27. *CF*, 37.
28. *CF*, 37-38.
29. *CD*, 54.
30. *CD*, 54-55.
31. Eberhard Bethge, "Freedom and Obedience in Dietrich Bonhoeffer," in *Prayer and Righteous Action in the Life of Dietrich Bonhoeffer* (Ottawa: Christian Journals Ltd., 1979), 54.
32. *CD*, 56-58. Bonhoeffer finds it even possible to speak of obedience serving a transitional role as a first external step in placing a person within a situation in which faith becomes a possibility. For this reason, although he denies that a person achieves his own conversion or justice, he can still recognize the freely willed decision to make an external act favorable to the faith situation.
33. *CD*, 50-52.
34. *SCH*, 178ff.
35. Bethge shows that the foundations for Bonhoeffer's theology of discipleship, as expressed in *The Cost of Discipleship*, were set early in 1932. See *DB*, 158ff.
36. See *CD*, 217ff., 232-233 *et passim*.
37. *CD*, 35.
38. *CD*, 44. The English translation has been corrected to read "ravens" instead of "eagles." The original German has *die Raben* which is best translated as "ravens."
39. Bonhoeffer describes the "volunteer disciples" who choose their own way of following Christ, those who must set their discipleship within a legalistic framework, and those who set conditions to their discipleship. In each instance, self-interest, not the person of Jesus Christ, is the prime motive and, for this reason, they are unworthy of the calling to Christian discipleship. See *CD*, 50ff.
40. *CD*, 89.
41. *CD*, 90.
42. *SCH*, 189.
43. *CD*, 80.
44. *CD*, 79.

45. *SCH*, 194ff. Clifford Green notes here that Bonhoeffer's statements on the misuse of power are, at times, an overreaction against the tensions of his own past. "Because his strengths had existed in the mode of autonomous power, he is trying to subject all autonomy to Christ's 'absolute authority' and power; hence the statements about weakness. But since he has not distinguished between mature and healthy ego strengths and selfish, dominating power, he is involved in the attempt to suppress the strengths of his ego—strengths which theologically and psychologically should be affirmed. There is thus a power struggle within himself. To a significant degree, we believe, this struggle is reflected in the statements about the authoritarian and combative power of Christ" (197).

46. *SCH*, 194.

47. *SCH*, 195.

48. *CD*, 159.

49. *BEM*, 65-66.

50. See "The Church and the Jewish Question," *NRS*, 221-240. On the question of Bonhoeffer's attitude toward the Jews and the Jewish question in Nazi Germany, see Ruth Zerner's well-documented essay, "Dietrich Bonhoeffer and the Jews: Thoughts and Actions, 1933-1945," *Jewish Social Studies*, 37, 3-4 (Summer/Fall 1975), 235-250. See also William J. Peck, "From Cain to the Death Camps: An Essay on Bonhoeffer and Judaism," *USQR*, 28, 2 (1973), 158-176; and *BEM*, 65-72.

51. *NRS*, 223. Historian Ruth Zerner wrote of Bonhoeffer's concern for his "Jewish brethren": "While Bonhoeffer's public statements in 1933 revealed the caution and restraint of a church leader conscious of his role in this community, his personal actions and private comments steadily revealed his concern for the plight of Jews in general. His personal letters show the depth of his concern for the 'sensible' people in the Church who 'completely lost their heads and their Bibles' in dealing with the Jewish question. The testimony of Bonhoeffer's Jewish-Christian friend, Franz Hildebrandt, is clear and unequivocal in relation to Bonhoeffer's support of Jewish-Christian clergy: Bonhoeffer 'reasoned, in view of the so-called "Aryanization" of the clergy under the Nazi laws, that he could not be in a ministry which had become a racial privilege. I cannot recall or imagine any other man to have taken this line of solidarity with those of us who had to resign their pastorates under that legislation.'" Zerner, *art. cit.*, 244-245.

52. *NRS*, 225-226.

53. "Die Geschichte und das Gute," *GS*, 3, 470.

54. *E*, 240 (trans. slightly altered).

55. *E*, 113-115.

56. *E*, 115. See also the essay, "After Ten Years," *LPP*, 4-6.

57. *E*, 261.

58. *E*, 240-241. See also Larry Rasmussen, *Dietrich Bonhoeffer. Reality and Resistance* (Nashville: Abingdon, 1972), 50ff.

59. *E*, 222-223, 258.

60. *E*, 238.

61. See *E*, 238-240, and the whole argument of Bonhoeffer's essay, "After Ten Years," *LPP*, 3ff.

62. *LPP*, 229-230.

63. *LPP*, 280.

64. *LPP*, 327.

65. *SCH*, 307-309. Green notes here that Bonhoeffer was finally able to make a clear distinction between mature strength and the misuse of power, criticizing power as authorities then wielded it to manipulate and dominate people, yet affirming strength as a capacity needed for self-fulfillment. The strengths he associates with autonomy and maturity are ego strengths, enabling the individual to exert leadership and responsiblity. From this, Dr. Green sketches an important biographical context of Bonhoeffer's prison theology: "Bonhoeffer, as a Christian, had now truly found freedom from the ambitiousness of self, and the competitiveness it entailed. This was true freedom because it no longer had to take the form of submission, renunciation and self-denial; it now had the form of serving and self-giving. In the resistance movement he entered into an authentic freedom for others. This fulfilled freedom then allowed him to affirm his own strengths, now with the confident knowledge that they were no longer self-serving; the suppression of the ego strength and autonomy advocated in *Nachfolge* was no longer necessary" (309).

66. See "The Madman" in *The Gay Science*, trans. with commentary by W. Kaufmann, Book 3, 125 (New York: Viking, 1974), 181-182. In misusing the philosophy of Nietzsche for their own ends, Nazi philosophers omitted the spiritual aspect of Nietzsche's humanism. Nietzsche's idea of the "superior man" was not limited to any one race.

67. Nietzsche had written: "The Christian conception of God—God as god of the sick, God as a spider, God as spirit—is one of the most corrupt conceptions of the divine ever attained on earth. It may even represent the low-water mark in the descending development of divine types. God degenerated into the *contradiction* of life, instead of being its transfiguration and eternal Yes! God as the declaration of war against life, against nature, against the will to live! God—the formula for every slander against 'this world,' for every lie about the 'beyond'!" From "The Antichrist" in *The Portable Nietzsche*, trans. W. Kaufmann (New York: Viking, 1966), 585.

68. See *E*, 33-37.

69. On this point, André Dumas comments that, "while Nietzschian freedom is a total protest against the deceptions of idealism, it is still without doubt a hatred of the reality of the neighbor. Dumas also quotes Karl Barth to the effect that Nietzsche was essentially "the prophet of . . . humanity without the fellow-man." See Dumas, *Dietrich Bonhoeffer. Theologian of Reality*, trans. Robert McAfee Brown (New York: Macmillan, 1971), 161-162.

70. "Thy Kingdom Come" in John Godsey, ed. and trans., *Preface to Bonhoeffer* (Philadelphia: Fortress, 1965), 34.

71. Ludwig Feuerbach, *Lectures on the Essence of Religion*, trans. R. Manheim (New York, 1967), 285.
72. Feuerbach, *The Essence of Christianity*, trans. G. Eliot (New York: Harper Torchbooks, 1957), 26.
73. See the letter of July 16, 1944, LPP, 360. On how Bonhoeffer uses the concept of God's paradoxical strength in weakness as an answer to Nietzsche and Feuerbach, see my article, "Bonhoeffer's 'Nonreligious' Christianity: Antecedents and Critique," *Bijdragen*, 37, 2 (April-June 1976), 118-148.
74. *LPP*, 286.
75. *LPP*, 281.
76. *LPP*, 327.
77. *E*, 248-249.
78. Letter of July 18, 1944, *LPP*, 362. Bonhoeffer's use of the words "religion" and "religious" is conditioned by the earlier critique of religion in the writings of Feuerbach, Nietzsche, and Barth and, therefore, signifies many things that are inimical to genuine faith: excessive introspection, thinking in terms of two spheres of reality, refusing to recognize the Christological structure of the world reality, efforts to manipulate God and to justify oneself, etc. The list could be broadened to include all the deviations and unfortunate cultural accretions that have set deeply into organized religion with the especially unfortunate result that people have often confused religion with both revelation and faith. His ambivalent use of the term has led to considerable confusion among his interpreters.
79. *LPP*, 369-370.
80. *LPP*, 327; see also *LPP*, 341-342, 344-346. We should keep in mind in examining Bonhoeffer's concept of the "world come of age" that the German word *mündig* means only that a person has come of age; it does not denote the full wisdom of adult maturity. See John Godsey, *art. cit.*, 84-85.
81. *LPP*, 327.
82. Letter of July 18, 1944, *LPP*, 361 (trans. slightly altered).
83. *LPP*, 382.
84. Maria von Wedemeyer-Weller, "The Other Letters from Prison," *USQR*, 23, 1 (Fall 1967), 26. The sentiments expressed in this letter are similar to Bonhoeffer's attempt to join the concepts of the blessing and the cross in his letter of July 28, 1944. "It is true that in the Old Testament the person who receives the blessing has to endure a great deal of suffering... but this never leads to the idea that fortune and suffering, blessing and cross are mutually exclusive and contradictory—nor does it in the New Testament. Indeed, the only difference between the Old and New Testaments in this respect is that in the Old the blessing includes the cross, and in the New the cross includes the blessing" (*LPP*, 374).
85. Letter of May 29, 1944, *LPP*, 312.
86. Letter of July 21, 1944, *LPP*, 369.

87. See *LPP*, 286, 327, 341, 361, 391-392; also the "Outline for a Book," where Bonhoeffer sketches the role of the church as a creative force within the world (*LPP*, 382-383).

88. See *E*, 297-298; also 131-132.

89. See *LPP*, 360, 361, 370.

90. *CF*, 82ff. Jørgen Glenthøj goes so far as to say that the problematic of *Creation and Fall* is the theme giving a continuity to Bonhoeffer's fragmentary but creative writing. See "Bonhoeffer und die Ökumene," *MW*, 2, 120.

91. *E*, 103. "There is the godlessness in religious and Christian clothing, which we have called a hopeless godlessness, but there is also a godlessness which is full of promise, a godlessness which speaks against religion and against the Church. It is the protest against pious godlessness insofar as this has corrupted the Churches, and thus in a certain sense, if only negatively, it defends the heritage of a genuine faith in God and of a genuine Church."

92. Letter of July 16, 1944, *LPP*, 360-361 (trans. slightly altered).

93. *E*, 240-241, 248-251; see also Larry Rasmussen, *op. cit.*, 32ff.

94. *E*, 238.

95. *E*, 243-245.

96. *E*, 240-241 (trans. slightly altered).

97. *BEM*, 125. In describing the dilemma of the conspirators, Bethge writes: "It is difficult in normal times to realize the unhappy state of divided loyalties which these men experienced, or to understand why the most conscientious person had to accept disgrace. In such a situation, however, the Christian proves himself to be a Christian. Normally, treason implies a base disposition and it is engaged in for personal advantage and with the intention of harming one's country. The opposite holds good for these men."

98. *E*, 241 (trans. slightly altered).

99. "After Ten Years," *LPP*, 3. Commenting on how this "devotion to duty" could be exploited by the Nazis for their evil ends, Bonhoeffer observed that the German "misjudged the world; he did not realize that his submissiveness and self-sacrifice could be exploited for evil ends. When that happened, the exercise of the calling itself became questionable, and all the moral principles of the German were bound to totter. The fact could not be escaped that the German still lacked something fundamental: he could not see the need for free and responsible action, even in opposition to his task and his calling; in its place there appeared on the one hand an irresponsible lack of scruple, and on the other a self-tormenting punctiliousness that never led to action. Civil courage, in fact, can grow only out of the free responsibility of free men" (*LPP*, 6).

100. "After Ten Years," *LPP*, 14.

101. *LPP*, 382.

Chapter 4

1. Paul-Gerhard Schoenborn, "Bonhoeffer and West Germany Today," *Newsletter. International Bonhoeffer Society for Archive and Research,* 14, (September 1978), 2.

2. *BEM,* 11.

3. *SC,* 37.

4. *SC,* 87-88.

5. *SC,* 87-88.

6. *SC,* 89.

7. *SC,* 90-93.

8. *SC,* 97.

9. *AB,* 122 (trans. altered from "communion" to "community").

10. *AB,* 123.

11. *WK,* 66 (also *GS,* 5, 269).

12. *AB,* 120.

13. *AB,* 121 (trans. slightly altered).

14. Barth had attempted in his theology to preserve a sense of God's freedom *from* man, that is, "bound by nothing," never manipulable by man. While Bonhoeffer agreed that God could not be "manipulated," he insisted that Barth's theology pushed God's freedom too much into the supratemporal and revelation into atomized, isolated units dependent on God's fresh interventions. God would then recede into his own nonobjective world of supernatural remoteness. In effect, Barth seemed to have described an eternally remote God forever eluding human grasp either by language or prayer. This for Bonhoeffer seemed too formalistic a presentation of God's freedom. The true picture of that freedom, Bonhoeffer argued, lies in his having made himself graspable in his Word, in Christ, within the church. Bonhoeffer indicted Barth's early theology of revelation for lacking the concreteness to which the Bible itself attests. See *AB,* 82-91.

15. *AB,* 123.

16. *AB,* 110.

17. See, for example, Ruth Zerner, "Dietrich Bonhoeffer and the Jews: Thoughts and Actions, 1933-1945," *Jewish Social Studies,* 3-4 (Summer/Fall 1975), 240.

18. See *E,* 205-206.

19. *CC,* 65.

20. *CC,* 65-66.

21. *CC,* 63-65.

22. *CC,* 66.

23. "What is the Church?," *NRS,* 155. The church is described by Bonhoeffer in this essay as being at once worldly and holy, a social institution and God's judgment on society, a religious organization and the communion of saints.

24. "Thy Kingdom Come," in John Godsey, *Preface to Bonhoeffer,* 29.

25. Ibid., 30.
26. Ibid., 45.
27. "On the Theological Basis of the World Alliance," *NRS*, 157.
28. "Thy Kingdom Come," in Godsey, *op. cit.*, 42-43.
29. *E*, 288. Bonhoeffer lists these mandates here as church, marriage and the family, culture, and government. Earlier he had labeled these four mandates as labor, marriage, government, and the church. See *E*, 207. He describes the difficulty of naming the "mandates" in a letter dated January 23, 1944. "Marriage, work, state and church all have their definite, divine mandate, but what about culture and education? I don't think they can just be classified under work, however tempting that might be in many ways. They belong, not to the sphere of obedience, but to the broad area of freedom, which surrounds all spheres of the divine mandates" (*LPP*, 192-193).
30. *E*, 201.
31. *E*, 301; see also *E*, 83.
32. *WK*, 21-22.
33. *WK*, 21-22.
34. Martin Niemöller, cited by Hans Knight, "The Holocaust," *Discover: The Sunday Bulletin*, Philadelphia, July 17, 1977, 7.
35. *NRS*, 225.
36. *NRS*, 226.
37. Ruth Zerner, *art. cit.*, 243. For a fuller development of Bonhoeffer's relationship to and defense of the Jewish people under Nazism, see chapter 6, especially notes 8-14.
38. *GS*, 1, 37.
39. *NRS*, 182.
40. *NRS*, 182.
41. *NRS*, 153-154.
42. *CD*, 228.
43. See my article, "An Interview with Jean Lasserre," *USQR*, 27, 3 (Spring 1972) 151-152; see also *DB*, 112-113.
44. *NRS*, 185.
45. The text of the Barmen declaration may be found in Arthur C. Cochrane, *op. cit.*, 237-247. Especially significant is the restatement of the theological premise of the association of the German churches which opens the declaration: "The impregnable foundation of the German Evangelical Church is the Gospel of Jesus Christ, as it is revealed in Holy Scripture and came again to the light in the creeds of the Reformation. In this way the authorities, which the Church needs for her mission, are defined and limited." On the basis of this, the declaration goes on to condemn the errors that were creeping into the church via Nazism. The first two of these errors, which in the text are prefaced by a positive affirmation from the scriptures and the church's confession are as follows: 1) "We repudiate the false teaching that the Church can and must recognize yet other happenings and powers, personalities and truths as divine revelation alongside this one

Word of God, as a source of its preaching"; 2) "We repudiate the false teaching that there are areas of our life in which we belong not to Jesus Christ but other lords, areas in which we do not need justification and sanctification through him" (trans. slightly altered).

46. The text of this letter can be found in *GS*, 1, 192-193. That Bonhoeffer was Bishop Bell's principal informant on the situation of the church in Germany is evident from an examination of their correspondence of the period. Bonhoeffer even helped him in drafting the text. See *GS*, 1, 182-191.

47. Bethge describes the difficult position in which Bonhoeffer was placed by his insistence on a rigorous attitude toward the German Reich church. "Bonhoeffer's position was a peculiar one. In spite of his whole-hearted partisanship, his brethren in the German Confessing Church had come to look upon him as an outsider because of his perpetual concern with the Sermon on the Mount. Yet among his ecumenical friends, to whom the Sermon on the Mount was of prime importance, he had become a stranger as a result of his insistence on the Confession and the need to repudiate heresy. He himself believed that the sterility threatening the confessionally based opposition to the usurpers must be offset by the Sermon on the Mount, while the Confession must be used to combat enthusiasm in the opposition which had based itself upon the Sermon" (*DB*, 298).

48. In an article published in *Evangelische Theologie* in August of 1935 and entitled, "The Confessing Church and the Ecumenical Movement," Bonhoeffer put the church struggle within the wider range of Christianity itself and obedience to the revelation in Jesus Christ, stating "that the struggle of the Confessing Church is bound up with the whole preaching of the Gospel, and . . . the struggle has been brought to a head and undergone by the Confessing Church vicariously for all Christianity and particularly for western Christianity" (*NRS*, 327). In the same article he explains the Confessing Church's refusal to enter into ecumenical cooperation with the German Reich Church in terms of the very struggle for Christianity itself. See *NRS*, 330.

49. Hence he turned down invitations to the conference in Chamby and to the "Faith and Order" gathering, both held in 1935. See *DB*, 546-550. Bonhoeffer's letters to Canon Leonard Hodgson who had sent the invitation to the "Faith and Order" gathering show him refusing to bend before the Canon's proposals to compromise. See *GS*, 1, 230-234. His grounds for refusing are principally the declaration of the Confessing Church, "that the Reich Church government has dissociated itself from the Church of Christ" (233).

50. See W. Visser 't Hooft, "Dietrich Bonhoeffer and the Self-Understanding of the Ecumenical Movement," *The Ecumenical Review*, 17, 2 (April 1976), 200. Bonhoeffer had himself written of the event in glowing terms. "It is just an expression of the true power of ecumenical thought that, despite all the fear, despite all the inner defences, despite all the attempts, honest

and dishonest, to disinterest the ecumenical movement, the ecumenical movement has shared in the struggle and the suffering of German Protestantism . . . when finally in the memorable conference at Fanö in August 1934, the ecumenical movement framed its clear and brotherly resolution on the German church dispute and at the same time elected the President of the Confessing Synod, Dr. Koch, to the Ecumenical Council. It was in those days that many leading churchmen for the first time came to see the reality of the ecumenical movement" ("The Confessing Church and the Ecumenical Movement," *NRS*, 327).

51. *BEM*, 85.
52. *NRS*, 159.
53. *NRS*, 160.
54. *NRS*, 283.
55. *DB*, 307.
56. *NRS*, 294.
57. *NRS*, 291.
58. *DB*, 313; see also *IKDB*, 90.
59. *NRS*, 327.
60. *NRS*, 334.
61. *DB*, 223-224. Bethge notes that, "all attempts to get the idea of an interdict accepted proved vain; very few people showed any understanding for the ideas of these two young men. The reaction was either one of indignation over such political intransigence or of failure to recognize the potential of such tactics. Indeed, the notion was not so illusory after all, for in 1941 the Norwegian clergy did not hesitate to lay down office in this way, thus securing a lasting victory." Bethge adds that for the first time both Bonhoeffer and Hildebrandt contemplated leaving their church.
62. *BEM*, 109.
63. *DB*, 411.
64. See Chapter 1, note 15.
65. *WF*, 93ff.
66. *WF*, 93-94.
67. *GS*, 2, 308.
68. *GS*, 2, 314.
69. *BEM*, 107ff.
70. *E*, 113-115.
71. *DB*, 466. Bonhoeffer's unwillingness to compromise on the issue of allowing representation from the German Reich Church, which he considered heretical, is brought out in an additional letter to Henriod. He stated unequivocally that his purpose was to frustrate the plan to have one of the Reich Church delegates present at the upcoming Oxford ecumenical conference. He informed Henriod that he was "fully aware that your only concern was to be just and to have a comprehensive representation of the German churches at Oxford. But my view is that such an arrangement,

although it may appear just in a formal sense, is in fact unjust and spiritually indefensible for reasons which need not be discussed here" (*DB*, 467).

72. *TP*, 198.

73. Hamish Walker, for one, pinpoints Bonhoeffer's venture from a theology of the incarnation to a theology of the cross as the source of his failure to make theological sense of the world in his *The Cost of Discipleship*. The world thus became something to separate oneself from. "At this period," according to Walker, "Bonhoeffer draws a tacit but far-reaching distinction between the world of persons and the world of things. This latter world is the fallen world of which Satan is the focus and inspiration. . . . Without saying so in so many words, what Bonhoeffer holds at this period is that this world of things is beyond redemption. The incarnation is not a full entry into the world in all its depth and richness. It is an extraction of humanity from the ambiguities of historical existence. It is a salvation of the world of persons and an implicit repudiation of the world of things. God's love may be universal in scope, but it is not sufficient in depth. The world is left out. It therefore remains for his theology of the cross to take up that unfinished business, and it does so as an act of sheer power unrelated to love." See Hamish Walker, "The Incarnation and Crucifixion in Bonhoeffer's *The Cost of Discipleship*," *Scottish Journal of Theology*, 21, 4 (December 1968), 413-414. I hope it will be clear from my own text why I view these assertions of Walker and others as somewhat gratuitous.

74. Hanfried Müller, *Von der Kirche zur Welt: Ein Beitrag zu der Beziehung des Wortes Gottes auf die Societas in Dietrich Bonhoeffers theologischer Entwicklung* (Hamburg: Herbert Reich Evang. Verlag, 1966), 244ff.

75. Ernst Lange, "Kirche für Andere: Dietrich Bonhoeffers Beitrag zur Frage einer verantwortbaren Gestalt der Kirche in der Gegenwart," *Evangelische Theologie*, 27, 10 (October 1967), 13.

76. Eberhard Bethge, "The Challenge of Dietrich Bonhoeffer's Life and Theology," *World Come of Age*, ed. Ronald Gregor Smith (Philadelphia: Fortress, 1967), 51-52.

77. *CD*, 252.

78. Müller, *op. cit.*, 246. For a more detailed debate with Hanfried Müller over his interpretation of Bonhoeffer, see my article, "Marxist Interpretations of Bonhoeffer," *Dialog*, 10, 3 (Summer 1971), 207-220.

79. See the chapter entitled, "Ministry," LT, 69-85; see also Bonhoeffer's "Article Explaining the Purposes of the Seminary," *WF*, 70-71.

80. "The work does not cease to be work; on the contrary, the hardness and rigor of labor is really sought only by the one who knows what it does for him. The continuing struggle with the 'it' remains. But at the same time the breakthrough is made; the unity of prayer and work, the unity of the day is discovered; for to find, behind the 'it' of the day's work, the 'Thou,' which is God, is what Paul calls 'praying without ceasing' (1 Thess. 5:17). Thus the prayer of the Christian reaches beyond its set time and extends into the heart of his work. It includes the whole day, and in doing so, it

does not hinder the work; it promotes it, affirms it, and lends it meaning and joy" (*LT*, 52-53).

81. *WF*, 42-43.
82. *WF*, 45-46.
83. *WF*, 47-48.
84. Letter of July 21, 1944, *LPP*, 369.
85. Certainly one reason for the strong eschatological emphasis of *The Cost of Discipleship* lies in his disappointment with the church reaction to the evils of the Hitler era. How this disappointment reached a near crescendo in Bonhoeffer's life forcing him into deeper alienation from his church is described rather well in Thomas Day's vigorous account of the events. Day notes: "The leaders of the Confessing Church were bent on compromise which amounted to capitulation. Bonhoeffer distanced himself from their position and opted for solidarity with the shrinking group of illegal young pastors who were being left to their fate. Then on 9 November, 1938, came the 'Crystal Night' of organized terror against the Jews. The church again remained silent. The beaten remnants of the Confessing Church seemed willing only to fight rearguard actions. More and more Bonhoeffer withdrew from the self-serving struggles of a church which would not be for the oppressed. Each church institution in which he had put hope and confidence had failed. However, he had always believed in and understood the church as personal community rather than as institution. 'What God wants to destroy, we will gladly have destroyed. We have nothing to save. We have not set our heart in structures and institutions, not even our own.' Bonhoeffer did not reject his church when it failed, but sought to follow Luther's example in taking on its burden, standing in with those of its members who would do what had to be done on behalf of the whole church which was failing its responsibility." See Thomas I. Day, *Dietrich Bonhoeffer on Christian Community and Common Sense* (New York and Toronto: Edwin Mellen Press, 1982), 116.
86. *E*, 197.
87. *E*, 198.
88. *E*, 199.
89. *NRS*, 104-105.
90. *NRS*, 117.
91. *NRS*, 246.
92. "After Ten Years," *LPP*, 6 (trans. slightly altered).
93. *BEM*, 125.
94. *BEM*, 72.
95. "After Ten Years," *LPP*, 5.
96. *E*, 115.
97. *E*, 114 (translation of pronouns referring to church has been altered from "she/her" to "it/its"; this translation change will be maintained in all subsequent quotations).
98. *BEM*, 118-119.

99. Letter of August 3, 1944, *LPP*, 378 (trans. slightly altered).

100. Ted Gill, "What Can America Learn from the German Church Struggle?" in Franklin H. Littell and Hubert G. Locke, *The German Church Struggle and The Holocaust* (Detroit: Wayne State University Press, 1974), 286.

101. Thomas Day, *op. cit.*, 203.

102. *LPP*, 382.

103. *LPP*, 382-383.

104. Bonhoeffer had developed the theme of suffering as a mark of the true church in *CD*, 272-273, and 76ff.

105. *LPP*, 361.

106. From Bonhoeffer's poem, "Christians and Pagans," *LPP*, 349.

107. *LPP*, 361. What Bonhoeffer meant by "participation in the sufferings of God in the secular life" must be examined in terms of Christ's power manifested in his weakness, in the victory of his resurrection achieved through his suffering and death. These aspects of the dialectic can never be separated. Otherwise we might have, as Clifford Green has observed, "the cult of an impotent God, with no capacity to transform human life, and no way in which Christ could be Lord of man in his *Mündigkeit.*" Green goes on to say that Bonhoeffer's emphasis on the weak Christ was an effort to do away with the "power of God of religion." In effect, this would also represent an attempt to force people to accept personal responsibility for life and thereby to find God at the very center of one's strength and maturity. "The cosmic screen on which religious man projects his fantasies of compensatory power," Green points out, "is chopped down. In religious weakness man looks to God to find power; in the Bible he finds not the power God, but the weak Christ. Christ sends him back to his own human strengths; precisely in these strengths—in knowledge, achievements, success, responsibilities, happiness—one is to find God, Bonhoeffer argues. Also, in removing the power God he is overcoming that immature *dependence* typical of religion; if religion reinforces man's weakness and dependence, Christian faith builds mature strength and independence. The weak and suffering Christ, then, is the ultimate critic of religion" (Green, *SCH*, 320).

108. *LPP*, 383.

109. *LPP*, 371.

110. George Bernard Shaw, "Common Sense about the War," in Warren S. Smith ed., *Shaw on Religion. Irreverent Observations by a Man of Great Faith* (New York: Dodd, Mead & Co., 1967), 60-61. Used by permission of the Society of Authors, London.

111. *LPP*, 381.

112. *LPP*, 382 (trans. slightly altered).

113. *LPP*, 300 (trans. slightly altered).

Chapter 5

1. *LPP*, 280 *et passim*.
2. See the last section of this chapter.
3. *DB*, 830.
4. *E*, 240ff.
5. *LPP*, 300 (trans. slightly altered).
6. The former expression is from *LPP*, 361; the latter expression is Bonhoeffer's euphemism for the Jews and other defenseless victims of Nazism. See *E*, 114.
7. *LPP*, 300 (trans. slightly altered).
8. *LPP*, 280ff.
9. *LPP*, 300 (emphasis mine).
10. The practice whereby the ancient church avoided mention of Baptism, the Eucharist, or the mysteries of faith in the presence of the unbaptized. On Bonhoeffer's use of the term, see Gisela Meuss, "Arkandisziplin und Weltlichkeit bei Dietrich Bonhoeffer," *MW*, 3, 70-71. See also my article, "Bonhoeffer's 'Non-religious' Christianity: Antecedents and Critique," *Bijdragen*, 37 (1976), 143ff.
11. *LPP*, 281 (trans. slightly altered).
12. *LPP*, 286 (emphasis mine). These are not the only places where Bonhoeffer mentions the *arcani disciplina*. Bethge states that "when we were students at Finkenwalde we were surprised when Bonhoeffer sought to revive this piece of early Church history of which we had never taken any notice" (*DB*, 784).
13. "Christian life is the dawning of the ultimate in me; it is the life of Jesus Christ in me. But it is always also life in the penultimate which waits for the ultimate. The earnestness of Christian life lies solely in the ultimate, but the penultimate, too, has its earnestness, which consists indeed precisely in never confusing the penultimate with the ultimate and in regarding the penultimate as an empty jest in comparison with the ultimate, so that the ultimate and the penultimate may alike retain their seriousness and validity" (*E*, 141-142).
14. *E*, 126.
15. *DB*, 785.
16. Paul Lehmann, "Faith and Worldliness in Bonhoeffer's Thought," *USQR*, 23, 1 (Fall 1967), 43.
17. Oskar Hammelsbeck, "Zu Bonhoeffers Gedanken über die mündig gewordene Welt," *MW*, 1, 55-56.
18. See *DB*, 785-786.
19. Larry Rasmussen, "Worship in a World-Come-of-Age," in A. J. Klassen ed., *A Bonhoeffer Legacy: Essays in Understanding* (Grand Rapids: Eerdmans, 1981), 278.
20. See my article, cited in note 10 above.

21. *LPP*, 282. The most perceptive analysis of Bonhoeffer's critique of the concept of religion is to be found in *SCH*, 309ff.
22. *SCH*, 318.
23. Francis X. Manning, *Religion and Ethics in the Theology of Dietrich Bonhoeffer, Bishop John Robinson, and Harvey Cox* (Doctoral Dissertation: Pontificia Universitas Lateranensis, Academia Alfonsiana), 1969, 449.
24. *WF*, 230-231.
25. *NRS*, 105-106.
26. *WF*, 240-241.
27. *WF*, 246.
28. Eberhard Bethge, "Freedom and Obedience in Dietrich Bonhoeffer," in *Prayer and Righteous Action in the Life of Dietrich Bonhoeffer* (Ottawa: Christian Journals Ltd., 1979), 65.
29. *LPP*, 371.
30. *TP*, 166.
31. *GS*, 3, 43.
32. *GS*, 3, 43.
33. *LT*, 77.
34. *WF*, 231, 246.
35. *LPP*, 391.
36. *LT*, 86 (trans. slightly altered).
37. *LPP*, 131.
38. *LPP*, 393.
39. *LPP*, 190.
40. *LPP*, 139-143. These prayers, along with Bonhoeffer's prison poetry, have been published as a collection, together with an interpretation of their meaning by Johann Christoph Hampe, in Dietrich Bonhoeffer, *Prayers from Prison* (Philadelphia: Fortress, 1979). In referring to this collection and to Hampe's interpretation, I will use the abbreviation, *PFP*.
41. *PFP*, 45.
42. *LPP*, 312.
43. *LPP*, 348-349; *PFP*, 26.
44. *LPP*, 361.
45. *LPP*, 371.
46. *PFP*, 46.
47. On this point and on the whole question of Bonhoeffer's spirituality, see F. Burton Nelson, "Bonhoeffer and the Spiritual Life: Some Reflections," *Covenant Companion*, 67, 11 (June 1, 1978), 3-5.
48. *Ibid.*, 5.
49. *DB*, 382-383.
50. *LT*, 48.
51. Bonhoeffer, *Psalms: The Prayer Book of the Bible*, trans. James H. Burtness (Minneapolis: Augsburg, 1970), 10.
52. *Ibid.*, 20-21.
53. Nelson, *art. cit.*, 5.

54. *LPP*, 370-371; *PFP*, 27-28.
55. *E*, 114.
56. *LPP*, 381.
57. *PFP*, 35. Hampe comments: "So this poem must also be read as a word to the church. He had always been complaining over the years that its horizons were too narrow, so he had to show it the way. He had to go where the storm was raging, to risk his life, to refuse the invitation to stay in America, where he would have been warmly welcomed, at the time of danger. He had to take part in the attempt against Hitler, above all by his dangerous journeys; he felt that the Christian should stand outside where 'they cried aloud in fear of death.' Even where the church of his time had protested, it had thought chiefly of itself and its pastors in prison, and much too little about Jews and political prisoners" (*PFP*, 84).
58. From "Der Tod des Mose" in *Gesammelte Schriften*, vol. 4, 2nd ed. (Munich: Kaiser Verlag, 1965), 613-620; translated by Robin W. Lovin in James W. Fowler and Lovin, *Trajectories of Faith* (Nashville: Abingdon, 1980), 183.

Chapter 6

1. *BEM*, 26.
2. *Ibid*.
3. *LPP*, 17.
4. *DB*, 155.
5. *E*, 114.
6. Alan Davies, *Antisemitism and the Christian Mind* (New York: Herder and Herder, 1969), 153.
7. William Jay Peck, "The Role of the 'Enemy' in Bonhoeffer's Life and Thought," in A. J. Klassen ed., *A Bonhoeffer Legacy. Essays in Understanding* (Grand Rapids: Eerdmans, 1981), 353.
8. This shift, as indeed the entire scope of Bonhoeffer's stand on the "Jewish Question" and his defense of Jews and Judaism, has been developed in Eberhard Bethge's masterful essay, "Dietrich Bonhoeffer and the Jews," in John D. Godsey and Geffrey B. Kelly eds., *Ethical Responsibility: Bonhoeffer's Legacy to the Churches* (New York and Toronto: Edwin Mellen Press, 1981), 43-96.
9. *Ibid.*, 70ff.
10. *Ibid.*, 69-70.
11. Pinchas Lapide, "Bonhoeffer und das Judentum," cited in Ernst Feil ed., *Verspieltes Erbe: Dietrich Bonhoeffer und der deutsche Nachkriegsprotestantismus* (Munich: Kaiser Verlag, 1979), 129.
12. Ruth Zerner, "Dietrich Bonhoeffer's Prison Fiction: A Commentary," in Dietrich Bonhoeffer, *Fiction From Prison: Gathering up the Past* (Philadelphia: Fortress, 1981), 155.
13. *E*, 89-90 (trans. slightly altered).
14. *E*, 115.

15. *E*, 84-85.
16. *LPP*, 7.
17. *E*, 360.
18. *NRS*, 225.
19. *E*, 135.
20. *E*, 130-131. The references to Julio de Santa Ana are from his article, "The Influence of Bonhoeffer on the Theology of Liberation," *Ecumenical Review*, 28, 2 (April 1976), 188-197.
21. *LPP*, 378.
22. *LPP*, 382-383 (trans. slightly altered).
23. Cited in *Gaudium et Spes*, No. 58, *The Documents of Vatican II*, ed. by Walter Abbot (New York: America Press, 1966), 264.
24. *Gaudium et Spes*, No. 42, in ibid., 241.
25. *Gaudium et Spes*, No. 69 in ibid., 278-279.
26. "The Church and Human Rights," *L'Osservatore Romano* (Engl. edition), November 13, 1975, 9-10.
27. Cited in Robert McAfee Brown, *Theology in a New Key: Responding to Liberation Themes* (Philadelphia: Westminster, 1978), 55.
28. *Ibid.*, 41-42.
29. See Larry Rasmussen, *op. cit.*, 132-146.
30. On the relationship of Bonhoeffer's life and thought to present-day liberation theology, see especially G. Clarke Chapman, "Bonhoeffer and Liberation Theology," in John D. Godsey and Geffrey B. Kelly, *op. cit.*, 147-195.
31. *NRS*, 104.
32. *GS*, 4, 180-181.
33. *E*, 59.

Discussion Questions

1 Bonhoeffer: A Witness to Christ

1. How would you explain the attractiveness of Nazism to so many segments of the German church? What church measures might have better counteracted the racial, dictatorial policies of the Nazi regime?

2. In a letter to his brother, Karl Friedrich, Bonhoeffer wrote: "I know that inwardly I shall be really clear and honest with myself only when I have begun to take seriously the Sermon on the Mount." He had also mentioned that one of the factors in his personal liberation from self-serving ambitiousness was a rediscovery of the Sermon on the Mount. What is there about this Sermon (Matt. 5–7) which could help us as Christians to be "really clear and honest" with ourselves?

3. Do you agree with Bonhoeffer's insistence on daily meditation in the preparation of the ministers for an apostolate involving church resistance within Nazi Germany and with his statement at the height of the war years that meditation must be "the crystallization of everything that brings order into my life, both inwardly and outwardly"?

4. What is your opinion of Bonhoeffer's decision to return to Germany in 1939? How does this affect his influence on the theology of Christian discipleship? Had he remained in the United States during the war years, would his influence have been the same?

5. In prison Bonhoeffer wrote that the church's traditional approaches to problems like Nazism and war were like "rusty swords." Is there any way in which this statement could be true today?

6. What are the implications of Bonhoeffer's farewell words to Bishop Bell: "This is the end, but for me the beginning of life"?

2   Christ, the Center of Liberated Life

1. In what way might Bonhoeffer be accurate in asserting that God's love extended in Christ reveals his concern to bring people out of their self-centered isolation into a community of mutual and loving concern? How does the Christian community help to bring a person out of tendencies toward egocentric isolation?

2. How would an appropriation of Christ's attitude to exist solely to serve others be related to true liberation?

3. What are the implications of Bonhoeffer's insight that within the Christian community others "become Christ for us in demand and promise"?

4. What is your opinion of Bonhoeffer's approach to Christology through asking not *how* the incarnation is possible, but "who is the man Jesus for us?"

5. Do you think Bonhoeffer's insistence on unflinching obedience to the "Commanding Christ" of the Sermon on the Mount was an adequate response to nazism? to the problem of committing oneself to the gospel in any age?

6. In what sense is there truth in Bonhoeffer's claim that Jesus Christ is the hidden center of all history and the structure of all reality? Would you agree with Bonhoeffer that the traditional opposites—natural-supernatural, profane-sacred, rational-revelational—have an original unity in Christ?

7. How would you answer Bonhoeffer's question, "Who is Jesus Christ really for us today?," in the period of World War II? Today?

8. What are the implications for a theology of liberation in Bonhoeffer's description of the weak and suffering God in Jesus Christ?

9. What do you find most meaningful in Bonhoeffer's description of Jesus as "the man for others"?

3   The Liberation of Faith

1. Do you agree with Bonhoeffer's contention that true autonomy becomes a possibility only when an individual is saved from his egocentric individualism and made aware of his responsibilities within the ecclesial-human community?

2. What is your reaction to Bonhoeffer's criticism of attempts to understand oneself from within one's own intellectual powers and to his remark that such efforts come to grief in narcissistic isolation?

3. How is Christ able to help a person overcome his or her alienation from God, from others, and from oneself?

4. Why is it so necessary in living with others to allow the other freedom to relate in true personhood without danger of being reduced to one's own self-image? In this connection, why would Bonhoeffer fear that in his theology and preaching he was "running only into a divine counterpart" of himself? Is such a fear healthy for faith?

5. Why did Bonhoeffer insist so much that faith is a "direct act," that it is intentionality toward Christ alone? How does genuine reflection on faith enter into faith?

6. What does it mean to be "free for God"?

7. What is the significance of Bonhoeffer's insistence in *The Cost of Discipleship* that *"Only he who believes is obedient, and only he who is obedient believes"*?

8. Is there anything wrong with performing actions with the *intention of acquiring faith?* Why was Bonhoeffer opposed to this attitude?

9. What is "cheap grace"? What is your reaction to Bonhoeffer's complaint that many of his fellow church leaders "have gathered like ravens around the carcass of cheap grace and there have drunk of the poison which had killed the life of following Christ"? Would such a statement be applicable to church members today?

10. How did Christians in Germany palliate their consciences during the days when Hitler's racist policies were being enforced and during the war years? Does this situation repeat itself today?

11. What are the implications for Christian faith and freedom in Bonhoeffer's statement: "When Jesus calls a man, he bids him come and die"?

12. Bonhoeffer claimed that a Christian must "shape history." In what way is this accomplished? Did Bonhoeffer and his fellow conspirators help to "shape" the history of Christianity?

13. How did the example of Jesus enable Bonhoeffer to enter "into the fellowship of guilt" in joining the anti-Hitler conspiracy?

14. In what way is Bonhoeffer's theology a possible answer to the atheistic critique of Christianity posed by Friedrich Nietzsche and Ludwig Feuerbach?

15. What did Bonhoeffer mean by his concept of the "mature life" to which he claims Jesus calls people?

16. How does one "suffer with God" at the hands of a "godless world"?

17. What did Bonhoeffer mean by his paradoxical statement, "Before God and with God we live without God"? Does such an attitude promote a greater sense of freedom in living out one's faith?

18. What is your reaction to what Bonhoeffer considered the crucial question of faith: "What do we really believe? I mean, believe in such a way that we stake our lives on it?"

4   Faith, the Liberation of the Church

1. What are some of the signs that a church may be following a "comfortable, middle-class faith" interested more in retaining power and privilege instead of living the gospel?

2. How would such an attitude make the church vulnerable to acquiescent support of an evil dictatorship like that of Hitler?

3. What is your reaction to that aspect of Bonhoeffer's early ecclesiology in which he attempts to avoid both the "historicizing" and the "religious" extreme in describing the nature of church? Explain each, particularly as they might be manifest today.

4. In what way is the reality of God's revelation related to the reality of church? What sense do you make of Bonhoeffer's words that the "being of revelation" is "the being of the community of persons, constituted and embraced by the person of Christ, wherein the individual finds himself to be already in his new existence"?

5. Is it possible for one still to claim that the church is "the center of history" or that the church could be a "hidden center" of the state?

6. How do church and state "limit" each other? In what way can or should the church "serve as deputy for the world"?

7. Why is war so incongruous with the Christian gospel? Is George Bernard Shaw's suggestion practical (see note 109)?

8. Is there any sense in which the following words of Bonhoeffer, written in 1932, may be true today? The church has no fixed location "because it wants to be everywhere and is therefore nowhere. It cannot be grasped and therefore cannot be attacked. It exists only in disguise. On the other hand, the church in forfeiting its own place can be found only in the privileged places of the world.... It has lost its sense of place. Now the church is hated for having occupied the privileged places ... among the bourgeois and that spurious conservatism which clings to the old ways of doing things.... Its religious services meet the needs only of the petty bourgeois. The needs of the business leaders, of intellectuals, of the enemies of the churches, of revolutionaries, are ignored. It has settled down in a swirl of worldly ceremonies and has itself become radically secularized" (see note 32).

9. Was Bonhoeffer accurate in saying that "the church was in very great trouble over the 'Jewish Question' "? What was the nature of that "trouble"?

10. Bonhoeffer claimed that the church of his day was "dead," because it viewed the world reality in terms of power and technological "progress" and not in terms of the gospel. Can such a claim still be valid today? How does the gospel view the "world reality"?

11. In the setting of the problems that beset our society, how would you rephrase Bonhoeffer's statement, "Christ encounters us in our brother, the German in the Englishman, the Frenchman in the German"?

12. Many thought Bonhoeffer's attitude toward the German Reich Church both unreal and intransigent. Do you agree? Why was he so opposed to any compromise on this issue? Was his suggestion that the churches proclaim interdict against Nazi Germany naive? What do you think would have been the result of such an action?

13. Bonhoeffer complained that in risky decisions the churches hid "behind resolutions and pious so-called Christian principles." Is this still true? Do we tend to do the same in our private lives?

14. Bonhoeffer once declared: "Peace must be dared. It is the great venture." What can the churches and individual Christians do to accept this challenge Bonhoeffer posed at Fanö?

15. Is it possible for an ecumenical gathering or movement to act, as Bonhoeffer hoped, as the one, universal church of Jesus Christ? What kind of unanimity is possible within the various Christian denominations in the face of evident

social injustice? Do you feel the churches could have done more in opposing the evils of the Nazi regime? What particular actions would you
have recommended? How would you relate such actions to individual
responsibility within the churches?

16. What are the implications for the church of Bonhoeffer's question: "Will
they [church synods] ever learn that majority decision in matters of conscience kills the spirit?"

17. In what way would the practices of prayer, worship, meditation, confession,
and personal sharing in a believing community, such as Bonhoeffer introduced to his seminarians at Finkenwalde, be an aid to a more effective
ministry in the world?

18. What is the danger of "thinking in two spheres"—the sacred as opposed
to the profane—in the church's ministry to and relationship with the world?

19. Is the American church as "unfree" as Bonhoeffer claims. In other words,
does his criticism of the American church have any validity today (see
note 89)?

20. In what way could the church have supported the conspirators against
Hitler? In what way can the churches support movements for liberation
today? Can this ever include the factor of violence?

21. What is your reaction to Bonhoeffer's "Confession of Guilt" on behalf of
the church? How would you compose a "confession of guilt" on behalf of
the church of today, or a "confession of guilt" on behalf of yourself?

22. Do you think the churches must share in the blame of responsibility for
the evils and atrocities of World War II? Explain.

23. How would you interpret Bonhoeffer's assertion that "the church is the
church only when it exists for others"?

24. What do you think of Bonhoeffer's project for the future of the Christian
church? Are there any practical ways in which the church can become
more Christlike?

5   Freedom and Discipline: Rhythms of a Christocentric Spirituality

1. How would one go about helping people today to realize the freedom that
characterized the mission and ministry of Christ?

2. What are the implications for religion and society in Bonhoeffer's contention that God does not supply all the answers to human suffering?

3. How was the example of Jesus a support in the conspirators' struggle against Nazism? Would Jesus' example be a force in the modern struggle against social injustice? Explain.

4. Has Bonhoeffer's prophecy that we "will once more be called so to utter the word of God that the world will be changed and renewed by it" (see text for the complete quotation) come true today?

5. Does Bonhoeffer's call for a "discipline of the secret" (*Arkandisziplin*) have any relevance within the contemporary church? When is it necessary for the Christian to maintain a "qualified silence" in religious matters?

6. Does Bonhoeffer's critique of "religion" hold today? Is there any validity to his distinction between faith and "religion"? Explain.

7. Why did Bonhoeffer lament the "lack of faith and freedom" in American churches? Was his complaint justified?

8. What did Bonhoeffer mean by his conviction that Christians had to enter into a "daily, personal fellowship with the crucified Jesus Christ"? Why would such a prayer of meditation be necessary in combatting an evil such as Nazism?

9. How can one maintain a balance between prayer in solitude and the strength in fellowship of a Christian community?

10. What is the value of intercessory prayer and prayerful support of one another within a Christian community?

11. What did Bonhoeffer mean by his poetic assertion that "Christians stand by God in his hour of grieving"?

12. What are the advantages of a *structured* life of prayer such as Bonhoeffer incorporated into his training of seminarians at Finkenwalde and into his own observances in prison?

13. What is there about the Psalms which enables them to be integrated so easily into one's personal prayers?

14. Read and discuss Bonhoeffer's poem, "Stations on the Road to Freedom." Are these "stations" actually stages in Bonhoeffer's own life? Do they apply to the lives of modern martyrs? What is the significance of his poetic phrase, "Dying we behold thee [freedom] revealed in the Lord"?

15. Discuss the ways in which Christ's sacrifice is liberating to our faith.

6   Bonhoeffer, Church, and the Liberation of Peoples

1. Is it still true that the stated priorities of churches at local and international levels are often a witness to the manner in which religions can appear to serve only their own security needs or become preoccupied with trivia? Explain.

2. Why is it that some Christian parishes seem so preoccupied with money? How can a parish function without a sufficient financial base? How can a parish maintain a balance between its commitment to be Christ to the people and its need to use funds for worthwhile projects? How does this accord with Bonhoeffer's opinion in his letters: "The church is the church only when it exists for others. To make a start, it should give away all its property to those in need. The clergy must live solely on the free-will offerings of their congregations, or possibly engage in some secular calling" (*LPP*, 382)?

3. Would you agree that careless church teaching and cowardly attitudes of church leaders have contributed to some of the evil besetting today's society? Explain. How would this bear on the present-day church opposition to nuclear warfare or to warfare in all its forms?

4. Are there Christian church leaders or, for that matter, Christian church-goers who still defend recourse to war to solve political problems between nations? If you disagree with them, how would you answer their arguments on behalf of going to war, say, for the sake of national defense?

5. What is meant by Bonhoeffer's observation: "We have for once learned to see the great events of world history from below, from the perspective of the outcast, the suspects, the maltreated, the powerless, the oppressed, the reviled—in short, from the perspective of those who suffer" (*LPP*, 17)? In terms of the people who are victims of oppression today, how would you describe that "perspective"?

6. Is Bonhoeffer accurate in his affirmation that persecution of the Jews is a denial of Christ and of what Christianity should stand for? Explain. Have the churches of today repudiated anti-Semitism? How effective has that been for the promotion of dialog between Christians and Jews?

7. What is the significance for Jewish-Christian dialogue in Bonhoeffer's refusal to blame the death of Christ on the Jews rather than on the Romans and all sinners, including Christians? In like manner, how do you react to his way of interpreting the Hebrew Scriptures and in his growing identification of Christ with Judaism, particularly in the plight of the Jews in the Nazi period?

8. How do you interpret Bonhoeffer's observation in his *Ethics*: "Western history is, by God's will, indissolubly linked with the people of Israel, not only in terms of origins, but also in a genuinely uninterrupted relationship. The Jew keeps open the question of Christ. He is the sign of God's free and merciful choice and of the repudiating wrath of God. . . . An expulsion of the Jews from the West must necessarily bring with it the expulsion of Christ; for Jesus was a Jew" (89-90)?

9. In what way does Bonhoeffer's challenge to the churches to abandon their flight from the world accord with the aims of liberation theology today?

10. If Bonhoeffer's theology is to be helpful to liberation theology, does this mean that the churches must engage in more direct confrontation with military dictatorships or political realms dominated by greedy oligarchies? What shape might such confrontations take? Would not such actions be risky for both churches and church leaders? If so, is the confrontation worth the risk?

11. In tracing the influence of Bonhoeffer in the "Movement of Church and Society in Latin America" (ISAL), Julio de Santa Ana remarks that a possible conflict of aims and ideologies within the group was resolved by appeal to Bonhoeffer's own rejection of both radicalism and compromise in favor of a Christian ethic in which Christ's incarnation, death, and resurrection give a balanced direction to one's social energies. Do you agree that this approach is helpful in today's movements for liberation in underdeveloped or exploited countries?

12. What do you think of the cooperation between Christian and Marxist revolutionaries today? Need their attitudes on social justice be incompatible? How would Bonhoeffer's rejection of "thinking in two spheres" (natural and supernatural, sacred and profane, world and church) help in such cooperation?

13. As this applies to liberation theology today, what does Bonhoeffer mean by his statement that "the church must share in the secular problems of ordinary human life, not dominating, but helping and serving. It must tell people of every calling what it means to live in Christ, to exist for others (*LPP*, 383)?

14. What is the proper mission of the churches in today's world? Does this necessarily include involvement in a nation's political life? in the lives of those who determine economic policies?

15. What do you think are the real sources of injustice in society? Do you think the churches can ever be effective in combatting injustice in the many forms it assumes today? What actions are proper for church as church in the struggle against societal evil?

16. Why did Bonhoeffer denounce the diplomacy and compromise tactics of the churches during the Nazi era? Is there any lesson to be learned from this? Is it correct to say that the churches have traditionally tended to cater to the affluent, the influential, and the powerful? Would you change this? If so, how?

17. How have the churches come to grips with the dilemma of people resorting to violence when the political powers ignore the "cry of the oppressed"?

18. Why is it a wrong assessment of Bonhoeffer's life and theology to use him to justify any and all violence in a just cause? What restrictions does Bonhoeffer put on the violence needed to overthrow a tyrannical government?

19. Are there times when recourse to violence, even in the name of justice or to counteract oppression, might be a pursuit of what Bonhoeffer calls "cheap grace"? Explain.

20. What is meant by Bonhoeffer's words in his *Ethics*: "It is with the Christ who is persecuted and who suffers in his church that justice, truth, humanity and freedom now seek refuge" (59)? Is this still true today? Explain.